FOREIGN AID AND
FOREIGN POLICY

THE ELIHU ROOT LECTURES

FOREIGN AID
AND
FOREIGN POLICY

by
EDWARD S. MASON

Published for the

COUNCIL ON FOREIGN RELATIONS

by

HARPER & ROW, Publishers

New York and Evanston

PREFACE

THE CHAPTERS that form this little book were presented originally as the Elihu Root Lectures at the Council on Foreign Relations in May 1963. The three lectures expanded into four chapters, but the substance has remained substantially unchanged. I am grateful to the officers of the Council who gave me this opportunity and to the members who were kind enough to lend me their attention. The book was written at the Center for International Affairs, Harvard University, created in 1958 to foster advanced study of basic world problems by scholars from various disciplines and senior officers from many countries. And I humbly pay my respects to that great American statesman whose name adorns this series.

EDWARD S. MASON

CONTENTS

FOREIGN AID AND
FOREIGN POLICY

INTRODUCTION

To discuss foreign aid as an instrument of foreign policy implies that foreign aid programs are shaped with the interests of the aid-giving countries primarily in mind. I believe that, on balance, this is true not only for the United States but for the foreign aid programs of other countries. But the term "interests" covers a wide spectrum of concerns and, of course, it does not follow that because the interests of the aid-giving countries are served, the interests of the aid-receiving countries are thereby denied.

Most of the aid provided by smaller countries, e.g., the Scandinavian countries and Holland, takes the form of contributions to international agencies. Partly, this is because of the difficulty and expense of building up a separate aid administration; partly, it flows from a desire to strengthen the United Nations and affiliated institutions as instrumentalities for the promotion of peace and security. Aid from the larger countries is predominantly bilateral, indeed, overwhelmingly so. Well over 80 per cent of the total flow of aid from the developed to the less developed world in 1962 was bilateral. In the case of the two largest aid contributors, the United States and France, the geographical distribution of aid suggests a primary interest in mutual security. But it is clear that, in this activity as elsewhere, France and the United States do not espouse precisely the same interpretation of mutual security. American assistance immediately after the war was channeled predominantly to Western Europe. The Far East and later South Asia and the Middle East then came to the fore. Recently, the emphasis has shifted to Latin America. French assistance has been directed consistently and in large volume to former French colonies in Africa.

The primary motivations of other aid-giving countries are less clearly tied to security considerations. Indeed, the Germans tend to become impatient with the heavy emphasis on political goals. They prefer a more business-like approach. But to hold that security considerations should not predominate is not to deny that interests of one sort or another are heavily involved. Agricultural surplus disposal, which accounts for a sizable fraction of U.S. aid, is primarily concerned with domestic interests. Japanese financial assistance is frankly tied to commercial aims. So also is the aid from a number of countries. All this does not mean, of course, that a purely disinterested desire to help less developed countries plays no part in inducing foreign aid appropriations. It enters into the aid programs of all countries and, in the United States, probably goes far to explain why the public opinion polls continue to show a majority in favor of aid despite the currently obvious distaste in Congress for the aid program. But interest tends to outweigh disinterest in this field as in so many others. And in any case, however one assesses the balance, a consideration of aid as an instrument of foreign policy necessarily focuses attention on the aims of aid-giving countries.

As an instrument of foreign policy, however, aid is a useless tool unless it can be assumed that there is a strong community of interest between the aid-giving and aid-receiving countries. As I have suggested, the political and other interests of the aid-dispensers have a good deal to do with the geographical distribution of aid. Apart from these geographical aspects, it might be somewhat difficult to detect the difference from an aid program shaped in the interests of the aid-receivers. If military assistance is involved, there is presumably a strong mutuality of security interests. If aid takes the form of economic development assistance, can a mutuality of interest also be assumed?

The interest of the aid-receiving country in economic development assistance presumably requires no demonstration. But what interests of the aid-dispensing countries are served in providing such assistance? There are obviously certain commercial considerations, but for the main aid-giving countries these are of minor importance. If the interests of these countries are thought to be served, it must be because the kind of a world in which the less developed countries are developing through our assistance is likely, in some significant sense, to be a more secure world than one in which they either remain largely stagnant or can advance only at the expense of a totalitarian mobilization of their own resources. This is an admittedly vague statement of objectives and, indeed, the political justification of aid is a subject that lends itself to relatively meaningless but usually resounding pronouncements. The current academic critics who assert that a political theory and political rationale for aid is almost completely lacking are in large measure correct. I have attempted to discuss the rationale of aid in Chapter 2. But I would have to say that the study of the connections between development assistance and economic development and between economic development and its political and social consequences is a very thinly cultivated field.

If there is some reasonable expectation that economic development assistance *can* make a significant contribution to the peace and security of the West, it is surprising how small a financial sacrifice the countries concerned are willing to make to this end. The total flow of long-term public economic assistance funds from developed to less developed non-Communist countries in 1962 was approximately $6 billion. Of this, the United States contributed about three-fifths. But one reaches a figure of $6 billion only by including at world market prices our shipments of agricultural surpluses, which represent primarily a domestic disposal problem, and a sizable volume of loans at close to commercial terms. If this total were reduced to its equivalent in grant funds, which is the only appropriate way to assess the sacrifice of resources made by the aid-giving countries, it would not amount to more than $2 billion to $3 billion. It seems probable that unless this sum can be approximately doubled within the next five or six years, a number of countries in which we now have serious commitments will not be able to maintain a significant increase in per capita incomes. One possible consequence—and indeed a rather likely consequence in some countries—may be a movement toward the kind of autocratic government deemed capable of wringing from a reluctant citizenry the sacrifices needed to make good a shortfall of foreign aid. On the whole, this type of political development seems unlikely to further our interests. If economic aid is considered to be an instrument of foreign policy, it seems really a rather small instrument to deal with such a very large problem. We should not be too surprised therefore if the results are somewhat commensurate with the effort expended.

The 60 per cent of the total economic aid effort that represents the U.S. contribution is approximately proportional to our share of total national incomes of the aid-giving countries. As a percentage of national income, a number of countries in fact exceed the U.S. contribution, and the contribution of France is more than double. So far as economic assistance is involved, there is then no strong justification for a U.S. complaint of inequitable "burden-sharing." If, however, economic assistance is considered only a part of a mutual security program whose financing includes military assistance and domestic defense expenditures, the picture changes. U.S. defense expenditures are approximately three times the sum of the expenditures of all other NATO countries, and we finance the greater part of overseas military assistance. The United States, in discussions of burden-sharing, would like to consider foreign economic assistance as part of a total mutual security program. But not all countries view economic development assistance in this light, and there are obvious differences of opinion as to what the requirements of mutual security really are. Hence the difficulties, discussed in Chapter 3, of reaching agreement on an equitable sharing of the foreign aid burden.

Although U.S. foreign aid is predominantly bilateral, there is one area of the less developed world where we have embarked on a regional enterprise. The Alliance for Progress, discussed in Chapter 4, is now only two years old and is obviously suffering from serious infantile disorders. The principal question in the future of the Alliance would appear to be whether there can be developed in Latin America a multilateral organization performing somewhat similar functions to those of the Organization for European Economic Cooperation during the period of the Marshall Plan. Unless this can be accomplished, the Alliance for Progress may merely serve as another name for a series of essentially bilateral programs in Latin America.

1

AID AS AN INSTRUMENT OF FOREIGN POLICY

I<small>F</small> WE are to consider foreign aid as an instrument of foreign policy, it seems appropriate to ask at the outset what is aid; what kind of an instrument is it; and what manner of policy is it designed to serve? It is obvious from the confusion attendant on the current aid debate, a confusion that appears to deepen every spring as May gives way to June and Congressional hearings on the annual aid bill progress, that there is substantial doubt in the public mind over why we are doing what we are doing and what we expect to get out of it. Everyone agrees that what this debate most needs is a clear statement of our aid objectives. I am not able to pretend that you are about to be given such a statement, but perhaps some of the relevant elements can be clarified.

From the beginning the discussions about the objectives of foreign aid have fluctuated between two poles. On the one side are those who regard aid as a relatively disinterested attempt to assist the poor countries of the world toward economic development. On the other are those who consider that the only possible justification of aid is its contribution, if any, to the security of the United States. This discussion goes back at least as far as the Marshall Plan. Was the Marshall Plan a magnificent example of American generosity, or was it a calculated, and successful, attempt to stem communism through the economic and political rehabilitation of Western Europe? In general the stoutest defenders of the aid program are those who believe that economic development assistance is and should be the primary objective. It seems probable that the public opinion polls which regularly show a majority of those polled in favor of aid, regardless of its unpopularity in Congress, are heavily influenced by the home-grown and home-spun American view that we ought to do something to help our neighbors. The severest critics tend to be those who see security as the sole justification and are doubtful as to how much security can be bought with foreign aid. But even those who view aid as relatively disinterested economic assistance recognize that political developments in the receiving countries do and should condition the flow of aid. And even those "realists" who emphasize security recognize generally that security in these days is a mutual affair requiring a consideration of the divergent interests of other countries in both the developed and the underdeveloped world. Consequently, it may be that the gap between these two poles of opinion is not as wide as is commonly supposed.

Let me develop somewhat further some of the complexities of aid considered as an element of mutual security policy versus aid as an element of economic assistance policy. Insofar as foreign aid is considered to be a part of a mutual security program, questions arise concerning the other participants, the size and character of their contributions, and the manner in which they conceive of security. In 1961, 86 per cent of all foreign aid was extended bilaterally. Of this bilateral aid, 98 per cent came from the members of the Development Assistance Committee of the Organization of Economic Cooperation and Development plus Australia and New Zealand. Most of these countries are joined with the United States in various military pacts. If we consider the question of equitable sharing of the aid burden, a matter that will concern us in Chapter 3, it makes a good deal of difference whether we treat economic aid as separable or inseparable from the area of mutual security. If it is inseparable, then economic aid to other countries becomes part of a total package of domestic defense expenditures, military assistance, and economic development assistance. The whole exercise of burden-sharing is put on a security basis and if, as is true, the United States bears more than "its share" of the domestic defense expenditures, there is a strong argument that Western Europe should bear a larger part of the burden of military and economic assistance to other countries. I do not wish to go into the merits of this argument here but merely to point out that if aid is considered solely as an instrument of security, aid policy tends to become an important aspect of our relations with our Western European allies.

If, on the other hand, we think of aid primarily as economic development assistance, another range of problems comes into view. All assistance supplied to other countries is, in one way or another, foreign exchange support. In this respect it makes little difference whether the assistance takes the form of project aid or program aid, or whether the lending is to cover the local currency component or only the foreign exchange component. Important policy questions are involved here, but essentially all aid consists in providing increased access to imports. But aid is only one way of providing this access, and the general level of aid that needs to be found to support a given rate of development depends on the trade earnings of underdeveloped countries, and hence on the commercial policies of developed countries, on the receptivity of underdeveloped countries to private investment, and on a number of other matters. We shall have occasion to examine some of the relations of trade and aid in Chapter 3 and some of the relations between aid and private investment in Chapter 4. Here I wish only to emphasize that aid considered as economic development assistance is inevitably connected with a number of other policies affecting the foreign exchange available to underdeveloped countries.

But whether we emphasize mutual security or development assistance as the objective of aid, there is a *sine qua non* of any sensible aid program, i.e., the ability of the receiving country to make effective use of whatever aid is provided for whatever purpose. This presupposes a set of policies, administrative capacities, and attitudes in aid-receiving countries without which foreign aid is irrelevant. Foreign aid is never more than a fraction of domestic resources available for defense or development and usually a small fraction. The main effort must come from the aid-receiving country, and in the absence of the will or the capacity to make this effort, aid may merely replace the domestic resources that might otherwise be available; it may merely make easier the flight of domestic capital from the country in question; it may postpone the initiation of necessary but politically difficult internal measures; or it may end up in the pockets of a corrupt bureaucracy. It is a suspicion—and in some cases more than a suspicion—that aid may have produced one or more of these results that has soured many people on the aid program. It follows that an acceptable rationale for foreign aid must concern itself not only with ends but with the conditions under which these ends, whatever they may be, may expect to be satisfied.

〄〄〄

So much for preliminaries. Let us now turn back to the questions asked at the outset concerning the meaning of aid and the nature of the aid instrument. That aid is not easy to define, and still less easy to measure is indicated by the experience of the Development Assistance Committee (D.A.C.) in Paris. After wrestling with the problem for several months, the Committee gave up the attempt and now contents itself with an estimate of the total flow of long-term financial resources to developing countries. In 1961 this flow added up to the rather impressive figure of $8.7 billion, of which nearly $6 billion was public and $2.75 billion private transfers. But private foreign investment has never been considered aid, however much it may contribute to economic development, and the public flows represent a very mixed bag. They include such items as ten-year loans repayable in hard currencies at seven per cent interest, P.L. 480 shipments valued at world market prices, and consolidation credits which involve no flow of new funds. All these may have some title to be called aid, but, if so, some aid is more "aid-like" than others.

We might as a first approximation advance the proposition that aid means a transfer of resources from the government or citizens of one country to those of another on terms that, from the point of view of the receivers, are easier than could be obtained on the capital market. This would exclude foreign private investment and suppliers' credit unless the terms on which these flows were made available were softened by reason of government schemes guaranteeing repayment or in other ways absorbing part of the risk. It would include, of course, in the private flows, grants, soft loans, and technical assistance from foundations, churches, and other charitable institutions. Such a definition would include most of the flow of funds from governments and international public institutions.

Even so, there is a great difference in the burden imposed on donor countries by a grant requiring no repayment of principal or interest and a ten-year hard-currency loan at seven per cent. Attempts have been made to take account of differences in terms by converting all loans to a grant equivalent. It is easy to do this given a schedule of repayments of principal and interest and an appropriate rate of discount. Thus a Development Loan Fund forty-year loan at three-quarters per cent interest with a ten-year grace period has a grant equivalent of $73 per $100 of loan if we use a seven per cent discount rate. By the same token, a ten-year loan at seven per cent has a grant equivalent of approximately zero.

It might be interesting to consider what the application of such a formula does to the relative position of the various D.A.C. member countries as contributors of foreign aid. Oddly enough, it doesn't do much to improve the position of the United States. If we take the undiscounted bilateral flow of funds in 1961 as a percentage of gross national product, Portugal surprises by occupying the first position with 2.59 per cent of G.N.P. France comes next with 1.88 per cent of G.N.P., and the United States is a relatively poor third with 0.94 per cent. Applying the formula moves Portugal from first to third place, and the United States from third to second. But France remains far out in front with 1.68 per cent of G.N.P. in grant-equivalent aid, while the U.S. contribution is 0.65 per cent.[1]

Appealing as the application of such a formula may be to tidy minds, it fails to take account of a number of considerations that affect the value of aid to the receiving countries. What does one do, for example, with P.L. 480 shipments? In the calculations of the Organization for Economic Cooperation and Development they are valued at world market prices. But if we try to estimate the value to the United States of shipments of agricultural surpluses, we would inevitably arrive at a substantially smaller amount. Suppose all current U.S. noncommercial exports of agricultural products were offered for commercial sale. The prices we would receive for wheat, cotton, and other products now in surplus would clearly be substantially less than world market prices. We might consider these lower prices an approximation of the "cost" to us of supplying the less developed world with P.L. 480 shipments, or we might attempt to refine the analysis further. But whatever was done to the calculations, we may be sure that any economic valuation would produce a figure substantially less than the world market price.

So much for the value of aid from the viewpoint of the aid-giving countries. If we consider the value of aid from the point of view of the receiving countries, another set of considerations are involved. Take, for example the question of aid-tying. The Administration claims that close to 80 per cent of all U.S. aid will soon be tied to U.S. exports. Other countries do not usually adopt such formal tying procedures as the United States, but it is interesting to observe that it is extremely rare for a European-financed project in the underdeveloped world to yield business

[1] In 1962 the United States, which had 58 per cent of the total gross national product of all D.A.C. countries, contributed 63.6 per cent of the aid transferred by these countries. France, with 7.2 per cent of G.N.P., contributed 13.2 per cent. Portugal, with 0.3 per cent of G.N.P., contributed 0.8 per cent.

for American contractors or exporters. While all the D.A.C. member countries are on record as favoring untied assistance, we may take it for granted, I think, that to the extent it is practicable to do so almost all aid is tied aid. This, of course, is one reason why aid frequently finds domestic support in what otherwise might seem to be unlikely quarters. But whatever the reasons for aid-tying, there is no doubt that it reduces the average value of the aid dollar to the recipients. It is difficult to estimate the amount of this reduction, and the impact of tying will obviously vary greatly from country to country, but World Bank experience on competitive bidding for generating, industrial, and transportation equipment indicates that there are large differences in procurement costs among countries.

Limitations on the receiving countries' choice of shipping is another form of tying. American ships carrying aid-financed commodities receive freight rates as high as three times the open-market rates. To the extent that U.S. aid requires shipment in U.S. ships, the value of the aid dollar is definitely reduced. Nor are these all the considerations that would need to be taken into account to arrive at a fair appraisal of the value of aid to receiving countries. French assistance goes overwhelmingly to countries in the franc zone, and so artificial are the prices of both exports to and imports from that zone that it is difficult indeed to estimate the competitive value of French commodity assistance.

It is impossible, as I have suggested, to find a formula that would take all these elements into account and reduce the total flow of funds to a grant equivalent in dollars the recipient countries are free to spend where they choose. But I might hazard the guess that if it could be done, it would boil the nearly $9 billion in total flow of funds from the developed to the underdeveloped world to a figure in the range of $2 billion to $3 billion. This is not, of course, to say that this reduced sum represents the net value to the receiving countries of the flow of capital from the developed world. In any kind of commercial transaction both sides are expected to gain, and underdeveloped countries may gain more, dollar for dollar, from private investment which has no element of aid than from government money on relatively easy terms. But $2 billion to $3 billion may be a fair appraisal of the "unrequited" assistance received by developing countries when all limitations on the use of funds are taken into account.

♠♠♠

LET US stop worrying, however, about such scholastic questions as the "real" value of aid to recipients and the "real" value of the burden to the aid dispensers, and talk about the characteristics of the U.S. aid program as a policy instrument. The totality of U.S. economic assistance embraces much more than the set of activities covered by the foreign aid bill.

The Export-Import Bank lends annually $500 million to $800 million gross on long-term, partly for economic development purposes. If we consider aid to be a transfer of financial resources on better-than-commercial terms, Export-Import Bank developmental loans qualify as aid though the Bank is by no means a loss-making concern. The Bank also on occasion is required to make balance-of-payments loans conceived to serve U.S. political purposes and, of course, acts as a supplier of credits and credit guarantees to U.S. exporters. Agricultural surpluses are disposed of under Public Law 480, and in recent years this type of aid has amounted to about $1.5 billion a year gross at world market prices. In some countries, the United Arab Republic for example, it is our principal aid instrument. The Peace Corps is a rapidly growing adjunct to the aid program though it is not a particularly expensive instrument nor, by the way, very closely articulated with other elements of aid policy. The Peace Corps expects to have 9,000 people in the field by the end of 1963 and 13,000 by the end of 1964. On occasion the Treasury Department gets into the act as a contributor to stabilization programs. Really critical foreign situations have a way of ending up in the White House and, if money is needed to handle the problem, there are several possible sources, including a special Treasury Fund. Some unkind people refer to these operations as "bail-outs" and observe that for certain countries, usually to the south of us, they have a way of recurring with distressing regularity. Finally, we must include in the broad context of U.S. aid programs our contributions to international agencies. In the fiscal year 1963 appropriations for this purpose amounted to $374 million, of which $150 million was included in the foreign aid bill while the rest represented either regular contributions to international agencies or special appropriations such as those for the Congo.

All of these flows of funds, of commodities, and of personnel are outside the activities covered by the foreign aid bill. In fiscal year 1963 appropriations under the aid bill were $3,900 million, of which $1,375 million was earmarked for the military assistance program and $2,525 million for economic assistance. With unexpended balances from previous years the economic assistance program of AID in fiscal 1963 approached $3 billion. If we exclude supporting assistance and the contingency fund which, as explained below, properly belong with military assistance, and add P.L. 480 shipments at world market prices, expenditures for the Peace Corps, net lending by the Export-Import Bank for development, and contributions to international agencies engaged in development lending and technical assistance, we arrive at a U.S. economic aid program that currently totals about $4 billion a year.

The major allocations in the existing AID program apart from military assistance are development loans, development grants, supporting assistance, the contingency fund, and contributions to the Social Progress Trust Fund administered by the Inter-American Development Bank. The principal justification of supporting assistance is to permit countries now receiving military aid to divert a larger part of their resources to military build-up. Most of this assistance plus some substantial part of the contingency fund, therefore, must be considered primarily as military aid. Development grants which total about $370 million this fiscal year are principally for technical assistance. There remains approximately $1,350 million for development loans and $170 million for the Social Progress Trust Fund. The latter is used in Latin America, mainly for so-called impact programs such as housing, education, and health.

As one surveys this somewhat sprawling edifice, certain observations suggest themselves. In the first place, although all these sources of funds have some title to be called foreign aid, there are also strong domestic interests to be propitiated. This is clear enough in the disposal of agricultural surpluses and in the financing of U.S. exports, but it also permeates other aspects of the total program. Secondly, one is struck by the variety of situations in which aid instruments are expected to be applied. Here it is expected to help in repelling actual or potential invaders, there it is used to shore up a government considered to be better, from our point of view, than available alternatives. In one place it is used to prevent a country from becoming excessively dependent on trade with or aid from a Communist country, and in other countries it is used for straight development assistance. (We shall return to this multiplicity of objectives presently.) Finally, one is impressed by the difficulty of molding these different agencies, institutions, interests, and sources of funds into a set of instruments that can be used effectively to promote *any* type of policy. This is a problem abroad where, however, considerable progress has been made over the last few years in building up, under the ambassador, country teams representing the political, economic, military, and informational elements of U.S. policy. It is a much more difficult problem in Washington. It is a problem further complicated by the fact that, on the one hand, aid programs in any particular country need to be coordinated with the activities of other countries and international institutions and, on the other, by the fact that Congress in enacting aid legislation increasingly—and sometimes for good reasons—adds limitations and conditions that must be observed in the administration of the aid program. One conclusion, relevant for foreign policy, emerges from all this. Whatever kind of policy foreign aid is expected to serve, many of the instruments available are not likely to be subtle, flexible, and convenient tools adapted to tactical use and rapid maneuver. There has to be some kind of aid strategy, slowly matured and not subject to change in response to sudden flurries and alarms.

But, before turning to strategic objectives, let us consider further some aspects of aid as a policy instrument with particular reference to the set of activities embraced within the foreign aid bill. I am particularly concerned with some of the relations between military and economic assistance, between capital transfers and technical assistance, and between bilateral and multilateral aid. (I postpone to the last chapter a discussion of the relations between the public and private sectors in aid programs.)

Military and economic assistance obviously compete for U.S. resources available for foreign aid. In many countries the question whether U.S. interests are better served by transferring resources from military to economic use or vice versa is continuously under review. But military and economic development programs in a particular country are usually to some extent also complementary and frequently can be made more so. Furthermore, the prospects of getting out of the military assistance business depends substantially on whether economic development is such as to permit recipient countries to assume a larger share of their own military burden. Consequently, it is a matter of importance to consider briefly these relationships.

The great bulk of military assistance flows to nine countries on the periphery of the Communist world. Apart from these countries, most of the remainder is allocated for the maintenance of rights to air or communications bases or for the training of troops in various parts of the world. The President's Committee to Strengthen the Security of the Free World (hereafter called the Clay Committee) thought that military assistance appropriations might be reduced to $1 billion within three years. Secretary McNamara considers this to be impossible before 1968, even if all goes well. Beyond this, a further reduction will depend not only on the military situation, particularly in Asia, but also upon the ability of countries now receiving military assistance to shoulder a larger share of the burden.

Their ability to shoulder a larger share of the burden obviously depends mainly on the rate of economic development they are able to sustain. Presumably this rate could be increased if some of the resources, both domestic and foreign, now put to military use were diverted to productive use. Thus, even on straight security grounds, the question emerges both in the recipient countries and in the United States whether it is better to emphasize short-run security considerations at the expense of longer term capacities, or to do the reverse. Obviously, in certain situations there is no choice. In Viet-Nam the danger is immediate and real. In other countries, however, the competition between economic development and military build-up creates an important set of policy issues for these countries as well as for the United States.

Consider the present situation in India. The Indian government has been considering doubling its military expenditures. This would mean an increase from roughly $800 million a year to roughly $1,600 million or, in other terms, an increase from three per cent of national income to six per cent. What this might do to India's development program is suggested by the fact that Indian savings available for development have been running at about eight to nine per cent of national income. But this is a problem not only for India. Equipping an enlarged and strengthened military force will involve a sizable importation of military hardware. The United States and Britain have already agreed to supply $120 million in equipment on an emergency basis. How much more will be required is not yet clear. Nor is the shipment of finished military items the whole story. If Indian plans call for the construction and equipment of plants for military production, there will inevitably be a heavy foreign exchange component. If the United States is asked to supply a substantial part of this foreign exchange component, will we do so in addition to our already large economic assistance to India, or will it be at the expense of economic assistance? Presumably our position as a supporter of both economic development and military build-up gives us a certain amount of influence in India on the allocation of funds between defense and development. How that influence should be used becomes an important policy issue for the United States.

Enough has been said to indicate that military assistance and economic development assistance compete to a certain extent for foreign aid funds. Usually military assistance wins out in this competition since it is substantially harder for Congress to quarrel with a military evaluation of military needs than with an economic evaluation of economic needs. But in the receiving countries military and economic assistance can also be complementary. It is obvious, that military roads and bridges can also serve civilian needs, and it is possible, with forethought, that they might also serve them better. It is also obvious that economic development may in certain ways increase immediate as well as potential military capacities. But the possibilities are much larger than that.

In many of the countries to which we extend foreign aid the army is the best organization in the country and frequently one of the most forward-looking. In my own experience, this is conspicuously so in Pakistan. It is a good organization in the sense that it attracts some of the best elements in the society and gives them a sense of discipline, *esprit de corps* and public service; it takes peasant boys off the farm and gives them an elementary education, a knowledge of English, and frequently some experience in the use of tools. The army in these countries is usually an important contributor of literate and semi-skilled personnel to the rest of the economy, and it could be made into a much more effective training center with a little thought and effort. Furthermore, there are possibilities of using the managerial skills of army officers, particularly engineers, in supervising surplus manpower in the construction of various types of public works. Obviously, there are limits to the extent the army can be used as an engine of economic development without injuring its capacity as a fighting force, but it is my impression that these limits are usually far from reached. The U.S. military assistance program is increasingly aware of these possibilities, and the strengthening of U.S. country teams has tended to bring military and economic elements in closer contact, but there is still some distance to go. In short, I have said enough to indicate there are complementary as well as competitive elements in the relation of military to economic development assistance.

Economic development assistance takes the form either of shipping capital items and commodities or of providing technical assistance. The capital and commodity items furnished by the AID administration are primarily financed by development loans, usually for long terms and at low interest rates. The technical assistance is normally financed by development grants. Given elementary precautions, there is substantially less danger of failure, in the sense of a demonstrable waste of resources, in project and commodity aid than in technical assistance. A project can be and should be carefully surveyed, and its priority established before a commitment is made. Commodity aid is presumably tailored to a development program that makes sense to AID people in the field and in Washington. Furthermore, project and commodity aid can be administered by far fewer people per dollar spent than technical assistance. The great majority of overseas personnel in AID missions is engaged in technical assistance, and books such as *The Ugly American* have conditioned us to shudder at what can happen with so many and such conspicuous Americans running around in the field.

There is, however, another side to the story. If the risks of failure are greater in technical assistance than in capital projects, the possibilities of smashing successes are also greater. We have all heard stories of effective malaria-eradication programs at the cost of a few cents per capita per year and of agricultural advice that has yielded three blades of grass where one grew before. Some of these stories are true. It now seems probable that the water-resources project in the western desert may add a few hundred thousand acres of land irrigated from renewable underground water supplies to Egypt's frighteningly small stock. The technical assistance on this project has been American from the beginning. If the ultimate results approach what currently seems possible, the profitability of this exercise in technical assistance could be calculated only in astronomical figures. I have no doubt that if one struck a balance between the successes and failures of technical assistance, the average result would be strongly positive. But the failures are frequent enough, and sometimes ludicrous enough, to provide a fairly continuous flow of good copy. In the field of weapons development we are sufficiently inured to failures interspersed among the successes to shrug off the former. Our attitude toward technical assistance in not so sophisticated. Yet the new and the unknown is probably as large an element in the one area as it is in the other.

The chance of failure, and a few examples of palpable failure, no doubt account for changing attitudes and an increasing ambivalence toward technical assistance as an instrument of foreign aid and of foreign policy. In the "brave new world" of President Truman's Point Four, all things seemed possible. Technical assistance was going to lift the underdeveloped world by its bootstraps without the need for large flows of capital. When these hopes were disappointed, there appeared on the scene the econometricians brandishing their savings ratios and capital-output coefficients. They proceeded to demonstrate that all that was needed to increase per capita income by x per cent per annum was a savings ratio of y, plus enough foreign exchange to permit domestic savings to be effectively invested. These experts too are now somewhat less vocal, and it is coming to be recognized that there are more things in economic development than are dreamed of in this philosophy.

In the meantime the actual practitioners of technical assistance have been learning something about the art. Among other things they have learned that concentration on a few projects is better than attempting to cover the country with many; that if technical skills are to be effectively transferred, it is a question of years not months; that the demonstration by one farmer to his neighbors that a new technique actually yields results is better than talking about the technique to a hundred farmers. There are many other things learned and still to be learned, and the whole experience in technical assistance of the government, foundations, and other organizations needs to be analyzed and the proper lessons drawn therefrom. Enough is now known, however, to make it clear that technical assistance, properly used, is an effective tool of economic development and deserves a place alongside capital and commodity aid as an instrument of foreign policy.

Well over ninety per cent of U.S. aid is currently bilateral involving negotiations primarily between the U.S. government and the government of a recipient country. The remainder consists of contributions to the International Bank for Reconstruction and Development (I.B.R.D.), the International Monetary Fund (I.M.F.), the International Development Association, the Inter-American Development Bank, and of regular and special contributions to a large number of United Nations entities. In this connection the question naturally arises whether, if foreign aid is to be considered an instrument of foreign policy, all the tools of the trade should not be in U.S. hands? The answer is quite clearly "No." Rather, the question in any situation in which there is a choice between bilateral or multilateral action is how U.S. involvement can be most effective.

There seem to me to be at least three circumstances that favor multilateral engagement. First, a situation may also be politically so sensitive that action by the United States is out of the question. A clear example is the Congo. I do not want to argue the Congo question at this juncture. But it seems obvious that if the United States had decided to go it alone, it would have cost very much more; the results inside the Congo would have been problematical; and the results outside the Congo in the form of attitudes and actions of surrounding African countries and of the opportunity thereby given to others to fish in these murky waters would not have been at all problematical.

Secondly, it is frequently the case that pressure to alter policies and practices inimical to stabilization and development can be brought much more effectively by an international institution than by the U.S. government. This was brought home to me during the three years I served as part-time advisor to the Plan Organization in Iran. During this period the United States was a sizable contributor of both military and economic assistance. I frequently observed U.S. officials wringing their hands over policies and practices of the Iranian government, but I rarely observed them doing much about it. Nor do I think they could have in so sensitive a political situation. This, however, was not true of the International Bank or the Monetary Fund. These institutions were ready to put money into Iran only under certain conditions, and they were in a position, therefore, to make certain of these conditions stick. Since the conditions were favorable to economic development in Iran—which was a primary objective of our own aid program—the Bank and the Fund were in fact serving U.S. interests by means that really lay outside the capacity of the United States to use. This question of the "strings" that can or cannot be attached to aid under what circumstances is obviously an important aspect of the subject of foreign aid as an instrument of foreign policy and is a matter that will be considered at further length in the next chapter.

Thirdly, under certain circumstances, the use of the multilateral device can become an effective way of reducing the U.S. share of the foreign aid burden. Since Chapter 3 is devoted primarily to the subject of burden-sharing, I shall limit myself here to a few figures. In 1961 the U.S. contribution to the total flow of public long-term financial resources to the underdeveloped world was slightly in excess of 60 per cent. (If P.L. 480 shipments were excluded, the percentage would be substantially less than this.) On the other hand, the U.S. contribution to international development agencies is a much smaller percentage. To most official U.N. agencies, including the Bank and the Fund, it is around 30 per cent. Our share in I.B.R.D. is 28.5 per cent and in the I.M.F., 27.4 per cent. To the International Development Association, it has been about 40 per cent. To the Inter-American Development Bank, it is about 42 per cent. Insofar as these instruments can be used for purposes in which U.S. interests go hand in hand with those of the other participants, it is a way of promoting American (or rather) mutual policy interests at lower cost. The same observation may be made with respect to the less formal consortia and consultative groups that have been organized in recent years to undertake financing of the development programs of various countries. This is a multilateral device for coordinating bilateral aid. So far as the United States is concerned, one of the advantages of the multilateral aspect is its impact on burden-sharing.

There is, then, an important role for multilateral aid and multilateral consultations as instruments of U.S. foreign policy. One caveat, however, needs to be entered. If U.S. contributions rise much above 40 per cent of total contributions, U.S. insistence on control increases and the suspicion of U.S. control becomes universal. In certain quarters in Washington there is concern lest our large contribution to international agencies not carry a commensurate degree of influence. There should be at least as great a concern lest U.S. influence become so preponderant as to destroy the multilateral character of the instrument.

These are some of the characteristics of aid as an instrument of foreign policy. Let us turn now to a consideration of the purposes to which this instrument may be put.

2

FOREIGN AID:
IN SEARCH
OF A RATIONALE

I MEAN by the word "rationale" in this chapter's title a statement of ends, and of means appropriate to the attainment of these ends, sufficiently persuasive to secure continuing support from Congress and the voting public. I emphasize Congress and the voting public though the initial formulation of an aid program must, of course, be undertaken by the administration. It is highly probable that a forceful President who believes strongly in foreign aid can muster more support than a weak President who does not. But Presidents come and go, and if foreign aid is to continue as an essential element of our foreign policy, there must be continuing support behind it.

Political support from certain quarters can be had for the asking. Farmers who want to dispose of agricultural surpluses, manufacturers who are given relatively easy access to various foreign markets through the tying of aid, consulting firms who do a large business with AID, and exporters who enjoy guaranteed credits can be expected to support at least certain parts of the aid program. But there must be more than this. And the more will not be forthcoming unless a majority of the public and of Congress is convinced that foreign aid is a useful and important element of foreign policy.

To say that a foreign aid program will not be continuously supported unless important interests of the United States are seen to be involved is not to deny that a humane concern for the well-being of other people has also had significant influence.[1] Humanitarianism as a fundamental motivation has certainly played an important role in the actions of individual Americans, whether under private or public auspices, in the underdeveloped areas of the world. It requires a certain amount of missionary spirit for a man to settle down in a primitive Ghanian or Indian village to teach the local farmers how to improve their agriculture practices even though that man is on the government payroll. The activities of American foundations and of religious and charitable bodies in providing technical assistance in underdeveloped areas has been conspicuous. The reaction to the Peace Corps among the participants and the general public has indicated a large reservoir of disinterested concern for the well-being of others. There is no doubt that these sentiments are reflected in substantial support for a foreign aid program without regard to national interests. It seems probable, consequently, that an aid program of some magnitude would be supported on relatively disinterested grounds. Indeed, if a relaxation of cold war tensions made possible a sizable reduction in military expenditures, this program might be substantial.

While recognizing the importance of these sentiments, however, it is impossible for one who has watched the maneuvers and has listened to the political debate that year after year precede the enactment of the foreign aid bill to avoid the conclusion that the predominant considerations have to do with the security of the United States. The foreign aid program is formulated and promoted in an administrative and political setting that is not very amenable to humanitarian considerations. The agencies of

[1] The next few paragraphs draw upon Chapter 1 of my book, *Promoting Economic Development: The United States and Southern Asia* (Claremont, 1955) and on my contribution, "Competitive Coexistence and Economic Development in Asia," to the American Assembly volume *International Stability and Progress* (New York, 1957).

government responsible for the programs have annually to justify them before a Congress concerned with demonstrating to its constituents that their interests are being served. An administration unable to show that taxes levied in support of foreign aid have some fairly direct relation to the economic interests of important political groups or to the safety of the state will have difficulty in continuing these programs—and, probably, continuing in power. Presumably this is the reason why the President, who, in his Inaugural Address used fine words to the effect that we favor foreign aid because it is the "right thing to do," as Congressional hearings on the aid bill approached, appointed an advisory group with the rather pretentious title of Committee to Strengthen the Security of the Free World.

It seems necessary to labor this point because in certain quarters there appear to be expectations that a sizable international program of assistance can be established without regard to the economic and security interests of the contributing countries. Two eminent European economists, for example, Gunnar Myrdal and Jan Tinbergen, envision aid as a twentieth-century extension in the international sphere of those principles of the welfare state that the last hundred years have witnessed in the domestic sphere.[2] Myrdal presents this argument in a set of propositions:

That in the "integrated" international society of the West there has been taking place over the last century, largely because of a revolution in moral ideas, a redistribution of income and an equalization of opportunity. The effect has been that most citizens have acquired a sense of participation in their society that has largely eliminated the significance of earlier class struggles.

That an "integrated" international society acquires a similar redistribution of wealth and income and of economic opportunity between the rich and economically developed economies of the West and the so-called underdeveloped areas of the world.

[2] Gunnar Myrdal, *An International Economy: Problems and Prospects* (New York, 1956), Jan Tinbergen, *Shaping the World Economy; Suggestions for an International Economic Policy* (New York, 1962).

That there is substantial evidence of a spread of the ideas and values necessary to bring this about.

Without questioning the change in moral ideas over the last century on what constitutes a "just" distribution of income and economic opportunities, it is pertinent to remark that such redistribution as took place was greatly facilitated by the shift in political power made possible by the spread of democratic practices and institutions. On the international scene there is as yet no political structure within which a shift of power from the "haves" and the "have nots" can take place.

There has been a good deal of discussion in recent years of the moral obligation of rich countries to contribute at least one per cent of national income to the economic development of poor countries. Indeed, in a number of Western European countries such a contribution has been set forth as a goal by leading political parties. As a matter of fact, if we consider any flow of public long-term financial resources as aid, certain countries have already exceeded that target. As I pointed out in the first chapter, Portugal's long-term public investment in 1961 amounted to 2.6 per cent of national income. But this outflow was almost entirely on commercial or close to commercial terms and was concentrated on Portugal's overseas possessions. That humanitarian considerations explain this generosity is doubtful. The flow of public funds from France amounted to nearly two per cent of national income. Although a large proportion of this flow is in the form of grants and soft loans, it goes overwhelmingly to the former French colonies in Africa and the objectives appear to be predominantly political. French participation in multilateral financial arrangements elsewhere in the world is marginal and on close to commercial terms.

Although German aid, including reparations payments, approaches one per cent of national income, the average terms continue to be relatively hard. Excluding reparations, grants amounted to only nine to ten per cent of the total flow of bilateral aid; and loans typically carry interest rates varying from three per cent to close to commercial figures. Recently some softening of these terms has been observable. From the geographical dispersion and the types of projects favored, it would appear that commercial considerations play a relatively important role in the German aid program.

The flow of public funds from the United Kingdom in 1962 fell substantially short of one per cent, and her loan terms until recently were relatively hard—the government borrowing rate plus a management charge. Rather more than half of British aid, however, is in the form of grants, and in 1963 an extension of grace and repayment periods has substantially reduced the effective interest rate on development loans. Bilateral aid, with few exceptions, goes to the colonies and to members of the Commonwealth.[3]

The public contribution of the United States, if P.L. 480 shipments are included, has run close to one per cent of national income in recent years, and a large fraction of these contributions has taken the form of grants or soft loans. There is no reason to suppose that the humanitarian influence in the U.S. aid program has not been as important as in other countries, which is to say not negligible, certainly, but also not predominant. The U.S. aid program is a reflection of world-wide responsibilities assumed after World War II, and both the size and geographical direction of aid suggests its political character.

If aid were in fact predominantly motivated by a disinterested desire to promote the economic development of poorer countries, there might be less difficulty in arriving at a consensus on the appropriate volume and equitable sharing of the aid burden. As it is, differences in security conceptions and divergences of commercial interests make this a difficult exercise, a discussion of

---

[3] On the attitudes in various European countries toward aid, see W. Friedman, "Methods and Policies of Principal Donor Countries in Public International Development Financing: a Preliminary Appraisal" (New York: 1962), Mimeo.

On the British aid program, see *Aid to Developing Countries* (London, Cmnd. 2147, 1963).

which will concern us in the next chapter. While it may become possible at some stage to consider aid as a normal instrument of the welfare state designed to promote an integrated international society, the evidence suggests that such a stage is not yet.

SSS

IF AID is to be considered as predominantly a political instrument, what kind of policy does aid serve? Let me recall certain points set out in the first chapter. To the extent that foreign aid is oriented toward a mutual security objective, it will be necessary to consider other conceptions of security than our own. To the extent that foreign aid is concerned with the economic development of underdeveloped countries, the relation between aid and other sources of foreign exchange needs to be considered. Aid is under certain conditions an alternative to trade and perhaps not always the best alternative. It should be recognized that aid must inevitably be a fraction, and usually a small fraction, of the resources available in the receiving country, either for military buildup or for economic development, and hence the efficiency of aid to serve whatever purpose it is expected to serve will depend on the capabilities of the country in question to mobilize its own resources. Finally, in view of the complexities of coordinating the various American aid-giving and international agencies, the possibly divergent interests of our allies, and the relations between foreign and domestic resources in the aid-receiving countries, foreign aid is not likely to be a subtle and flexible instrument adapted to tactical use.

Recently there have appeared some highly critical and, on the whole, useful evaluations of foreign aid from scholarly quarters. I refer in particular to the observations of Hans Morgenthau of the University of Chicago and of my colleague, Edward Banfield, at Harvard.[4] These appraisals point out: (1) that a well-developed political theory or political rationale of foreign aid is almost completely lacking; (2) that the economic development of another country is not, from the point of view of the United States an end in itself but must be related to some significant American interest; and (3) that it by no means follows that economic development, even if it can be brought about through the agency of foreign aid, will serve significant U.S. interests. The basic difficulty with the aid program, according to this analysis, is that it denies the "sovereignty" of political interests.

I, for one, admit the sovereignty of politics in questions of foreign aid and ask only what are the political interests we should attempt to attain. During World War I, Clemenceau discovered that war is too important an affair to be left to the generals. Hans Morgenthau has recently discovered that foreign aid is too important a matter to be left to the economists. But, as I read his learned history of the uses of political bribery and their possible application to the current scene, I find myself wondering whether foreign policy is not too important to be left to political experts. He contrasts the political sophistication of the Soviet aid program with the naïveté of our own. "The classic example of this error is the American rejection of the Afghan request for paving the streets of Kabul as economically unsound. It may be noted in passing that the Soviet Union, pursuing a politically oriented policy of foreign aid, paved the streets of Kabul, even though that measure had no bearing upon the economic development of Afghanistan."[5]

Perhaps this was a classic error; I do not know. But to demon-

[4] Hans J. Morgenthau, "Preface to a Political Theory of Foreign Aid," *American Political Science Review*, June, 1962; reprinted as Chapter 28 of *Politics in the 20th Century* (Chicago, 1962). Edward C. Banfield, "American Foreign Aid Doctrines," first published in *Public Policy*, Graduate School of Public Administration, Harvard, 1961; Later a revised and enlarged version was published by the Amercan Enterprise Institute, Jan. 1963.

[5] *Politics in the 20th Century*, vol. III, p. 261.

strate it was an error, it would seem incumbent on Morgenthau to tell us what political advantage the Soviet government got out of its paving project as against the American advantage in building a hydroelectric dam. All that he says about this is that the power project was unknown to most Afghans and did not produce results for several years.

There is, in fact, continuous pressure to use foreign aid for tactical political purposes. Much of the aid thus used is, in my opinion, wasted. Every American ambassador, even the ambassador to the Upper Volta, finds it useful to have an aid program which he justifies on political grounds. It makes it easier to talk to the minister of finance, and it promotes good relations with other government officials. It does not follow that the United States has important interests that need to be served in Upper Volta. Diplomats are frequently worried by voting records in the United Nations and suggest that an increase in aid to their particular country would improve this record. But countries usually vote in the United Nations in ways their interests—or what they consider to be their interests—dictate. And if this does not permit the United States to accomplish its purposes through the United Nations, there are other channels. Some ambassadors, having established workable relations with a particular government, tend to think that the interests of the United States will be adversely affected if this government falls, and they bombard Washington with pleas for more aid, lest it in fact fall. I do not say that foreign aid cannot and should not be used for immediate and short-term political advantage. But I deny that this is the main, or even a very important, justification for aid.

One does not have to recognize immediate tactical advantage as the primary purpose of aid in order to concede the over-all primacy of political ends. The principal purpose of foreign aid in my view is to promote the security of the United States and, insofar as our security is dependent on others, foreign aid is an essential part of a mutual security policy. In certain under-developed countries this requires assistance in the form of military hardware plus enough economic assistance to permit these countries to mobilize their own resources for military use. In others the essential objective of U.S. foreign aid is the support of governments able and willing to maintain their independence of Communist control.

To say this is hardly more than to paraphrase the statement of goals in the most recent summary presentation to Congress of the *Proposed Mutual Defense and Assistance Program.* This is a clear expression of essentially political aims. "The several economic and military programs authorized by the Foreign Assistance Act are directed toward a single goal: To assist other countries that seek to maintain their independence and to develop into self-supporting nations."[6]

The political objective is obvious in what is called the strategic assistance program embracing military assistance, supporting assistance, and the contingency fund. These programs account for nearly half of the total request for funds for foreign aid for fiscal year 1964, $2,140 million of a total of $4,525 million. Three-quarters of military assistance flows to nine countries on the periphery of the Soviet Union and China, and most of the remainder is allocated to military training programs and to expenditures designed to secure military and communication facilities for American use. Well over half of the $435 million requested for defense support is designed "to strengthen the military-economic position of four countries on the fringe of the Communist bloc."[7] Military assistance and at least this portion of defense support are properly described as "strategic assistance" and are instruments of the long-term security policy of the United States. Changes in the size and composition of the assistance will come with changes in our appraisal of the strategic situation. Indeed, such a change has occurred in 1962–63 with respect to military assistance to India. But very little of this assistance is devoted to immediate tactical objectives.

[6] *Proposed Mutual Defense and Assistance Programs,* F. Y. 1964, p. 1.
[7] Same, p. 62.

The same thing cannot be said of the remainder of supporting assistance and of the uses to which the contingency fund may be put. Here we are concerned with immediate tactical objectives, and expenditures under these categories ordinarily make no significant contribution either to military strength or to long-term economic development. These funds go in general to countries beset by economic and political instability (nations in which the United States has a strategic interest), to countries that are excessively dependent on Soviet aid, and, in the case of the contingency fund, to meet unforeseen situations in which the security of the United States may be involved. In fiscal year 1962 the major uses of the contingency fund were the support of counterinsurgency activities in Southeast Asia and the meeting of emergency economic needs of politically vulnerable countries mainly in Latin America and the Middle East.

It is open to question whether military assistance and defense support are always used with maximum effectiveness. The Clay Committee questioned whether in certain Far Eastern countries we were not supporting local forces excessively large for purely defense purposes and in other areas helping to maintain establishments of little military value. It is also possible to criticize certain uses to which the contingency fund has been put. One wonders whether, on occasion, when United States ambassadors have pressed the case for emergency economic assistance lest the existing government fall, it might not have been better to let this happen. But these are matters of judgment in which strong differences of opinion can be and have been mustered. There is no doubt at all that with respect to that part of the foreign aid program designated as strategic assistance the objectives are essentially political. The security interests of the United States and of the free world are clearly involved, and it is this part of the program that tends to meet least resistance in Congress.

When we turn to what is called economic development assistance we enter a different realm of discourse. So far as the Agency for International Development is concerned this includes appropriations for development grants, for development loans, and for the Alliance for Progress. Appropriations for these categories amounted to $1,929 million in fiscal year 1963 and the administration request for fiscal 1964 totals $2,167 million. As I attempted to make clear in the first chapter, the AID funds for economic development do not by any means account for the total U.S. foreign aid program. It is necessary to add P.L. 480 shipments which, valued at world market prices, have been running at about $1.5 billion a year; expenditures for the Peace Corps which, in fiscal 1963, amounted to about $70 million; net loans of the Export-Import Bank for development purposes; and U.S. contributions to the International Bank and other U.N. agencies. Altogether the size of that segment of the U.S. foreign aid program that might properly be called economic development assistance in 1963 was approximately $4 billion.

It is, however, mainly AID appropriations that are subject to serious controversy. P.L. 480 shipments and Export-Import Bank loans are closely tied to domestic economic interests. The Peace Corps is a small and generally popular program. And U.S. contributions to the International Bank, to the International Development Association, and to other U.N. agencies concerned with economic development ordinarily meet with little Congressional resistance.

The opposition to AID appropriations for economic development assistance focuses principally on three issues. First, is it possible through external economic assistance to promote a type and rate of economic development in underdeveloped areas such that in the not-too-distant future the aided countries will become independent of external assistance? Or are we, in certain countries, engaged in a task of Sysiphus which can never be carried through to completion and, in others, because of governmental inefficiency and corruption, the unwillingness of privileged groups to make necessary social and economic concessions, or for other reasons simply throwing money "down a rat hole?"

Second, assuming that external assistance can make a necessary contribution to self-sustaining growth, is this likely to be accompanied by a process of political development such that, at a minimum, a country's independence of Communist influence is significantly strengthened? Under more favorable circumstances, are such countries likely to become members, in the words of the AID *Program Guidance Manual,* "of a community of free nations cooperating on matters of mutual concern, basing their political systems on consent and progressing in economic welfare and social justice?"[8] If the essential rationale of the aid program is political, what political consequences favorable to the United States and to the free world are likely to emerge from economic development?

Third, even if we assume that the economic and political consequences of economic development assistance are favorable to the interests of the free world, are we not bearing too large a share of the burden? If P.L. 480 shipments at world market prices are included the United States accounts for approximately 60 per cent of the total flow of long-term public funds from the developed to the underdeveloped countries in the free world. Furthermore, the terms on which we supply assistance are notably softer than those of any other country except France.

A discussion of the problem of "burden sharing" will occupy us in the next chapter; here we are concerned with possible economic and political consequences of external assistance. Obviously this is much too large a subject for the compass of this slim volume. Furthermore, it needs to be said that much too little is known about the process of economic development and the relation of economic and political development to permit firm pronouncements. All I can pretend to do is to interpret some of the experience of our fifteen-year history of foreign economic assistance and to offer a few reflections on the problem of formulating public policy in an area of great uncertainty. It must be recognized, however, that foreign economic assistance is not the only area in which action—or inaction—has to be undertaken on the basis of an inadequate knowledge of the consequences. One

[8] Agency for International Development, *Program Guidance Manual,* Aug. 1, 1962, p. 1.

has only to mention "test-ban agreements," proposed weapon systems, or, indeed, almost any area of current security policy. Our strictly national experience in foreign assistance begins with the Marshall Plan, and this experience serves to emphasize a distinction of increasing importance in the administration of U.S. aid: namely, a distinction between situations in which external assistance is a necessary and sufficient condition for economic development and situations in which it is a necessary but not a sufficient condition. The countries of Western Europe at the end of World War II possessed all the requirements for recovery and continued development except that of command over foreign exchange needed to replenish their stocks of working capital, to repair and replace destroyed production facilities, and to make it possible to restore the flow of intra-European trade.[9] This the Marshall Plan provided. Most of the underdeveloped countries now put forward by the Agency for International Development as "success stories" belong pretty much in the same category.

In addition to the Marshall Plan examples, Japan, Spain and Lebanon are cited as countries in which "economic aid has ended, because the countries concerned are now able to move ahead on their own."[10] In Spain and Lebanon foreign aid did little more than supply welcome quantities of foreign exchange. In Japan the American occupation was accompanied by various institutional changes, of which land reform was undoubtedly the most important. But with or without land reform there is no doubt that Japan, given initial assistance in the form of import financing, was ready for renewed economic development.

A second group of countries is described as "approaching self-sustaining growth and the day when economic assistance can be

---

[9] The extent of U.S. intervention in domestic policies to assist economic recovery in Western Europe will be considered in Chapter 4 in connection with a discussion of the Alliance for Progress.

[10] Statement of David E. Bell, *Foreign Assistance Act of 1963*, Hearings before the Committee on Foreign Relations, United States Senate, 88th Cong., 1st sess., p. 68.

terminated."[11] This group includes Greece, Israel, Free China, Venezuela, and Mexico. U.S. assistance to Venezula and Mexico has been marginal. If and when these countries are judged to have entered on the path of "self-sustaining growth," it will not be the result of any substantial external assistance. Development aid to Greece, Israel and Free China, on the other hand, has been massive. In fact, these three countries, along with Jordan, stand at the top of the list in terms of economic assistance per capita during the period 1946–62. The rate of economic development in recent years has been highly satisfactory, if not spectacular, in all three countries. There is no doubt that massive foreign aid was a necessary condition to development. Indeed, without such aid it is doubtful whether any of the three would have survived as independent countries. But it is probably correct to say that massive foreign aid was not only a necessary but a sufficient condition for economic growth. This is perhaps less true of Greece where U.S. influence on domestic economic policy was particularly strong. But in all three countries a high level of investment initially underwritten by foreign aid is now financed by domestic savings, the marginal savings rate is high, and all have gone far toward overcoming chronic balance-of-payments difficulties. Yugoslavia would also have to be added to the list of countries in which the conditions of growth were present, and all that foreign assistance could and did supply was access to increased imports.

A third group of countries, including India, Pakistan, Turkey, Nigeria, and Columbia, are described as "following sound developmental policies and making good progress, although they are not yet so close to the date when aid can be ended." There are also a number of countries—Chile is mentioned as an example —in which our main concern is with developmental assistance but where, "given past performance, assistance must be conditioned on improved performance." Altogether there are some thirty countries in which it is said the "U.S. effort is directed to solid and lasting economic and social development." These coun-

[11] Same, p. 69.

tries absorb approximately three-fourths of current U.S. economic assistance.[12]

There are seven countries, including Korea and Viet-Nam, in which our primary interest is described as the maintenance of "external and internal security with economic development as a long-run goal." Finally, there are some forty-odd countries to which U.S. aid is marginal because other countries, as in the franc zone, are principal contributors, or because of marginal strategic significance, or, possibly, because it is judged that developmental prospects are dim.

A good deal of thought has been given in recent years, both within and outside the AID, to the process of economic development and how this process should influence the allocation of developmental assistance. One result of these cogitations has been a certain concentration of assistance in countries in which development prospects are favorable. A second result has been a closer examination of the conditions, over and above the provisions of foreign exchange, necessary to development and of the extent to which the United States, using whatever instruments are available, can influence aid-receiving countries to meet these conditions. The primary focus of this attention has obviously been in the thirty-odd countries which are the main recipients of developmental assistance. As I have emphasized above, the countries that either have moved or are about to move beyond the need for further aid are, in general, countries for whom the provision of increased access to imports is a necessary and sufficient condition for economic development. The others range from countries in which such access over a longer period of time may be sufficient, to countries in which something more than this is definitely required.

What is this "more"? In certain countries it may be the introduction of policies conducive to monetary stabilization, and a viable exchange rate. In others, it may be "self-help" measures designed to increase the contribution of local resources to de-

[12] Same.

velopment. In some, various social reforms including land reform may be called for. To what extent is it possible and desirable, using whatever leverage is provided by foreign aid, to influence domestic policies in the direction of economic growth?

SSS

To RAISE this question is to introduce the controversial question of the "strings" that may or may not be attached to aid, a subject on which a lot of nonsense has been written. The demand in many underdeveloped countries is for "massive aid without strings." But aid is never supplied without conditions of some sort. The only questions worth discussing are what kind of conditions, imposed by whom, and under what circumstances?

The United States has long ago, after a number of unfortunate experiences, given up the attempt to condition aid upon the acceptance of mutual security obligations. There remains, of course, the question whether our aid to countries allied in various security pacts should be more generous than to countries considering themselves to be "nonaligned"? The currently most critical situation is presented by India and Pakistan. Despite the large volume of economic assistance now flowing to India and recent and prospective military assistance contributions, aid to Pakistan on a per capita basis is still a multiple of that provided to India. Certainly U.S. aid policy has become more flexible with respect to the political attitudes of recipients, but massive aid per capita still goes in the main to countries which are joined with us in various security arrangements.

Aid continues to be used in various countries with immediate political objectives in mind. U.S. pressure surely had something to do with the disappearance of the Rhee government in Korea. Our unwillingness to give further support to the Diem regime in Viet-Nam prepared the ground for its overthrow. There was a period immediately after the war when governmental policies in Greece were highly responsive to U.S. suggestion. Military assistance to India appears to be accompanied by the discovery of a greater mutuality of interest than economic aid was ever able to invoke. In addition to these and other examples a substantial amount of U.S. aid, as I have suggested, has the short-run political purpose of preventing excessive dependence on Soviet sources of supply, influencing behavior in the United Nations or other forums, or keeping in power government deemed more favorable to our interest than feasible alternatives. I have also suggested that aid is frequently not a very useful instrument for these purposes. Since the ultimate goal of aid is, in my view, essentially political, it is not the political orientation of these uses of aid that I question, but merely the appropriateness, in some cases, of the instrument used in relation to our long-term objectives.

Here, however, we are primarily concerned with economic strings in the provision of assistance to those countries in which we are attempting to promote economic development in the interest of longer term objectives. Many of the conditions affecting the use of aid are laid down by Congress in the enabling legislation. Some, such as the provision requiring technical and financial planning for projects proposed for financing, are designed to assist aid administration in a wise direction of the funds entrusted to them. Others, such as the section of the Act requiring notification to U.S. small business of AID financial procurement, are designed to achieve essentially domestic objectives. A number of provisions are intended to prevent aid from going directly or indirectly to politically unacceptable countries. In the 1962 legislation a section was added—the so-called Hickenlooper amendment—which requires the President to suspend assistance to the government of any country which nationalizes or expropriates U.S. property without adequate compensation. Many of these conditions are intended to increase the effectiveness of aid and none of them, including the Hickenlooper amendment, which I shall discuss later, can be said seriously to impair the usefulness of aid to the recipient countries.

Much more significant is the increased tying of aid to U.S. procurement, which is a condition imposed by the administration rather than by Congress, though, of course, Congress would certainly legislate in this area in default of what it considers to be effective executive action. When aid is tied both to specific projects and to U.S. procurement, it is particularly restrictive. General balance-of-payments support, leaving the receiving country relatively free to choose the commodities to be procured in the United States, is considerably less restrictive. Nevertheless, despite the fact that tying tends to lessen the value of the aid dollar, there has been substantially little complaint of this type of string.

Arguments appear when economic assistance is used as a lever to attempt to bring about changes in domestic policies thought by aid administrators or others to be conducive to development in the recipient country. With respect to U.S. attempts to tie economic strings to aid, the receiving countries are distributed in a wide spectrum with India at one end and various Latin American countries at another. The American attitude toward Indian development policies and programs has, to date, been extraordinarily permissive. We have tended to take the various Five Year Plans and the accompanying policies as given and to concern ourselves with the problems of providing the required external financing. I shall return presently to the question whether we can or should take a different attitude. In Latin America, on the other hand, we have frequently engaged in tough bilateral bargaining in an attempt to bring about substantial changes in domestic economic policy as a condition of further assistance. I shall discuss some aspects of economic assistance under the Alliance for Progress in Chapter 4. In between the Indian and Latin American examples there are various degrees of permissiveness.

The U.S. aid administration has been willing to accept Indian plans and programs without much cavil largely because the Indian government has shown itself willing to make a serious attempt, at considerable sacrifice, to mobilize the country's own resources, because the planning effort has on the whole been careful and intelligent, and because in an economic situation of almost unparalleled difficulty India has made substantial progress. This does not mean that conditions have not been imposed on particular projects: indeed in all countries it is much easier to attach strings to projects than to program assistance; the conditions, after all, are limited to particular installations and do not adversely involve policies affecting the economy as a whole. Furthermore, they are typically of a sort that would accompany any sensible bank loan and consequently have an acceptable familiarity. Nevertheless, conditions connected with project assistance can, on occasion, extend to more general policy areas.

Negotiations in 1963 on possible AID financing of the proposed Bokaro steel mill in India is a case in point. Investigations by a team of experts from U.S. Steel pronounced the project technically possible but suggested that raw material reserves be fully proved before final decisions were undertaken. It was proposed, and accepted by Indian negotiators, that not only the construction but the management of the enterprise be in foreign hands for a considerable period of time. It was also suggested that shares be sold to private investors, which the Indian government has been loath to do in the case of other public sector enterprises. Finally, the negotiations seriously called into question many aspects of the Indian government's price policy with respect to iron and steel. In other words it had been made clear that if financing were to be available at all a number of conditions would have to be met.[13]

---

[13] Since Bokaro entered largely into the deliberations of the Clay Committee and since it has been actively discussed in Congressional Hearings, it seems advisable to add a few words on this subject. There is the question whether a public sector enterprise of this size could be expected to perform better or less well than a private-sector enterprise of similar size in India. (A smaller enterprise in the private sector would probably have been possible, given willingness on the part of the Indian government to offer the same guarantee for a D.L.F. loan as were contemplated for a public sector plant.) There is also the question whether, given existing ideological preconceptions in India

Nevertheless it is in connection with program assistance that the question of economic strings arises most significantly. Program loans and grants are intended to finance all or a substantial

---

and the United States, the proposal of such a large public sector loan would be likely to have an adverse effect on aid appropriations in general and on aid to India in particular.

It would have to be said that, on the first question, the evidence is inadequate. The management of public sector enterprises in India, with a few exceptions, leaves much to be desired. But it is also true that private sector management of large enterprises in India is rather conspicuously weak. The costs of various types of iron and steel products at private plants, where comparison is possible, are usually substantially lower than in public plants. But the capital costs at private plants installed at an earlier period are much lower than current replacement costs, and the public sector plants have still not been broken in. My guess is that, given foreign management during the running-in period, the efficiency of a public sector plant would compare favorably with a new plant of similar size in the private sector.

On the second question there is no doubt in my mind that ideological preconceptions, in the sense of sets of strongly held opinions that bear little relation to the ascertainable facts, enter on both sides. It is difficult both in India and the United States to hear a sensible discussion of the pros and cons of the public-private enterprise issue. On Bokaro it is argued on the one side that the United States in its foreign aid programs should not attempt to impose its ideological views on other countries. But as the Report of the Clay Committee put it, somewhat crudely and bluntly, "countries which would take this [the public enterprise] route should realize that while the U.S. will not intervene in their affairs to impose its own economic system, they too lack the right to intervene in our national pocketbook. . . ."

The reaction to Bokaro in the United States was occasioned not only by the fact that this was to be a public sector enterprise, but also by the size of the proposed commitment. The foreign exchange costs of the first phase were estimated at $500 million; and for the whole project spread, it is true, over eight or nine years, the foreign exchange cost was estimated at over $900 million. AID continually and without question lends for railway expansion, power plants, port facilities, irrigation works, and other enterprises in the public sector in India and elsewhere. Furthermore, the Export-Import Bank has financed publicly owned steel mills in Chile and Brazil. This latter financing, however, was on close to commercial terms, and the amounts were a small fraction of what is proposed for Bokaro. In recent years, U.S. economic aid to India, apart from P.L. 480, has been running at from $450 to $500 million a year. At least $250 million of this is for compart of the external costs of a set of projects plus the "maintenance" imports of spare parts, raw materials, and equipment needed to keep existing installations in operation. A program is normally part of a development plan that assesses the internal and external financial and physical requirements needed to attain certain goals and then proposes the allocation of resources and the policies and administrative measures designed to mobilize these resources and put them to effective use. Obviously the external resources needed and the effectiveness of their employment will depend, among other things, on the sacrifices the receiving country is willing to make in mobilizing its own resources and on the policies and practices affecting their use. Consequently aid-supplying countries, concerned as they are with the effective use of their own contribution, have a natural and legitimate interest in the domestic policies and practices that will affect this use. Questions arise, however, concerning the extent to which this interest justifies or permits intervention in what probably will be regarded as the internal affairs of the receiving country.

If the aid-dispensing countries were in the position, say, of a bank interested only in the financial prospects of the enterprise and the security of its advances, conditions could be imposed and the aid either dispensed or withheld, depending on whether the conditions were accepted and met. Some aid-dispensing countries, e.g., Japan, are in approximately this position and limit their "aid" to project-lending on close to commercial terms. The situation changes, however, when aid takes the form of financing the

---

modity support, leaving perhaps $200 million for projects. If Bokaro had been accepted, it would, during certain periods of construction, absorb approximately the whole of project assistance, assuming aid to India did not increase. This, without more, assured Bokaro a very high visibility whenever aid to India was discussed.

The decision has now been taken to withdraw Bokaro from further AID consideration. Whatever the political repercussions in India, not to have done so was to risk a flat Congressional prohibition. It would appear that ideological considerations are political facts of life that are not to be ignored with impunity.

external costs of a development program the success of which is likely to be affected by a long series of domestic actions, and when the ultimate objectives of aid involve political and security (rather than purely commercial) interests. It is impossible with respect to all the countries dependent on U.S. aid to make broad generalizations concerning the appropriateness and effectiveness of "strings" attached to economic development assistance. Nevertheless certain observations seem justified.

First, serious intervention in the domestic affairs of an aid-receiving country is not likely to be considered at all unless it is clear that without a significant change in policies aid will be unable to make a contribution to development. This has been considered to be the situation in a number of Latin American countries where, without some type of stabilization program, foreign assistance could be expected to be frittered away. Even under these circumstances a pronounced change in policy must be seen to be necessary not only by the aid-giving but also by the aid-receiving country. There is little room for imposed solutions in negotiations of this sort.

Secondly, it is usually much easier to bring about changes in domestic policies through the mediation of an international agency such as the International Bank or the Monetary Fund than through tough bilateral bargaining. The I.M.F. has been associated with most of the stabilization arrangements in Latin America. The consortium meetings presided over by the International Bank have come to be the most important forums for criticism of the development programs and policies of India, Pakistan, and other countries financed in this manner. The technical staff of the Bank in preparation for these meetings, and frequently at the urging of consortium participants, has been moving away from exclusive concern with the feasibility of particular projects toward an examination of practices and policies that bear on the effectiveness of the development program as a whole.

Thirdly, if the United States, or any other aid-dispensing country, is to exert influence on the domestic policies of an aid-receiving country, either directly or via an international agency, its representatives must have a clear idea, based on careful analysis, of what it wants this country to do. Frequently such ideas have been lacking. Recently AID has given increased attention to this problem and has attempted to formulate for some of the principal aid-receiving countries a so-called Long-Range Assistance Strategy which spells out U.S. economic, political, and security interests in the countries in question, the conditions necessary to their attainment and the relevant instrument of foreign policy. But it is a strategic, not a tactical instrument that, to be effectively used, requires over time a coordinated adaptation of external assistance from all sources to a set of domestic policies capable of mobilizing local resources and putting them to productive use. It implies external assistance without strings to countries whose own efforts are serious and promising. But it also implies in countries where "self-help" measures are deemed inadequate a disposition to attach conditions to aid somewhat stronger than has been traditional in AID policy to date. Such a strategy will necessarily be limited by immediate political and security interests in certain countries. But in the areas to which our economic development assistance mainly flows a carefully formulated assistance strategy tactfully applied holds some promise of accelerating the attainment of a situation in which continued aid is no longer a condition of economic growth.

This discussion has been focused on the thirty-some countries to which our economic development assistance mainly flows. All of these countries are to be considered capable, at some stage, of self-sustained growth. Some are in this situation already, and others are on the verge of reaching it. These and a few others, which are still some distance away from this goal, are, by and large, countries for which a temporarily increased access to imports and technical assistance has been or is a primary condition to the attainment of self-sustaining growth. This is not to deny that institutional changes or changes in domestic policies have made a contribution to development in some of these countries, nor is it to deny that further changes might have made an even greater contribution. But in the countries in question institutions, policies, and practices were and are sufficiently oriented toward growth to permit external assistance, without much more, to have a significant effect. Other countries in this list of thirty-odd, are seriously handicapped by failures—of varying degrees of seriousness—in self-help measures to put domestic resources to effective use. In some—perhaps Brazil is an example—economic growth seems almost impervious to domestic mismanagement. In others it is by no means impervious. In all of them, however, external assistance is unlikely to be effective unless it is accompanied by domestic change. The ability of an aid-giving country to condition its assistance on the achievement of domestic reforms is strictly limited. Nevertheless, there are ways of influencing domestic policy without attempting a degree of intervention that would be considered to be intolerable. And unless these can be effectively exploited there is indeed a danger that external assistance will disappear down the proverbial rat hole.

But, supposing external assistance is so used as to bring about significant progress toward the economic goal of self-sustained growth, what then? How are U.S. political and security interests, which are the primary objectives of aid policy, likely to be affected? As suggested earlier in this chapter, the current formulation of aid policy would appear to envisage a minimal and a maximal objective. The minimal objective can be stated as follows: "to assist other countries that seek to maintain their independence and to develop into self-supporting nations." More ambitious aspirations have frequently been stated in official foreign aid pronouncements, including that quoted above from the 1963 AID *Program Guidance Manual*; i.e., to assist in the development "of a community of free nations cooperating on matters of mutual concern, basing their political systems on consent and progressing in economic welfare and social justice. Such a world offers the best prospect of security and peace for the United States."

It is quite possible that such a world would in fact offer the best prospect of security and peace for the United States. But it is rather difficult to understand how economic development, no matter how expertly guided from abroad, can be expected necessarily to produce nations that will cooperate "on matters of mutual concern," political systems based "on consent," and societies "progressing in economic welfare and social justice." I would suppose that free nations would cooperate with the United States to the extent they conceive it is in their interest to do so and not much further. We do not have to look further than France to discover where cooperation is not all that the United States would desire. The Senate Hearings on the Foreign Assistance Act of 1963 were full of denunciations of French ingratitude and noncooperation. But surely it is better for our security and the security of the free world to have an independent France than one dependent on the Soviet Union, as appeared quite possible in the period before the Marshall Plan.

Whether emerging governments in the underdeveloped world are likely to represent political systems based on consent is a matter of interpretation. Every government needs a minimum of consent in order to govern at all. And no government can dispense with authority, which means that consent is never complete. In between is a rather wide spectrum, and I think we would be well advised not to press our own views of the meaning of political consent too far. Already there are a number of one-party systems in Latin America, Africa and Asia, and over the next few years it seems probable there will be more. The same thing can be said about economic welfare and social justice. These words have different meanings in different parts of the world, and it is perhaps wise not to be too parochial. In the long run governments will not be able to maintain their independence from Communist control unless they can offer their people an alternative that somehow seems better than communism. Recent experience in Iraq, Syria, Guinea, Ghana, and in other parts of the world suggests, moreover, that in general newly independent countries are not particularly eager to accept Communist tutelage if alternatives are indeed available.

The relatively firm basis on which a foreign aid program can and should be built seem to me to be the demonstrated facts (1) that in at least a large part of the less developed world foreign aid can make and has made an effective contribution to economic development; and (2) that most countries, developed and underdeveloped, desperately want to be independent of external control. The link between these two facts is provided by a proposition for which there is substantial evidence, namely that favorable prospects for economic development have significant relevance for the ability of countries to maintain their independence. In certain countries an alternative to Communist control can be considered only if actual or impending attack from Communist centers of power can be resisted. This is the situation in Southeast Asia, and foreign aid must necessarily take the form primarily of military assistance. In most of the underdeveloped world, however, the danger is not so immediate. Here the problem essentially is to keep open the possibility, and to encourage the unfolding, of a process of economic and political development that offers a real alternative to Communism.

This kind of rationale for a foreign aid program will not please all people. In fact it will definitely displease at least two types of critics. To those who would like to envisage aid as essentially a humanitarian effort to assist the underdeveloped world without regard to political considerations, it will seem niggardly and self-centered. To those who regard the primary justification of aid as the bringing into being of a group of countries committed to act with the United States and the West, it will seem inadequate. But in the world in which we live it is hard for me to envisage an alternative rationale close enough to the realm of the possible and to our own long-range interests to command continuing support.

3

THE PROBLEM OF
EQUITABLE SHARING OF
THE FOREIGN AID BURDEN*

As I suggested in the preceding chapter the three principal issues on which the U.S. foreign aid program meets attack, both in Congress and outside, concern first, the question whether we have contributed or can contribute notably through external assistance to the economic development of the underdeveloped world? Are we not, to coin a phrase, pouring money down a rat hole? Second, even if we can and do promote economic development, what interest of the United States is thereby served? Are we simply contributing to strength which, if not used against us, will not be conspicuously for us? Third, even if it can be shown that economic assistance promotes development and that development brings with it independence from Communist control, if not a willingness to cooperate with the United States, aren't we paying too large a share of the cost? As the United States confronts an increasingly serious balance-of-payments problem with a lagging growth rate while Western European countries, assisted by the Marshall Plan, have now become highly solvent and obviously capable of doing more, the problem of burden-sharing has tended to move into the center of discussions of the foreign aid program.

It was much to the fore in the Senate Hearings on the Foreign

* Certain parts of this chapter have already been published under the title "The Equitable Sharing of Military and Economic Aid Burdens," in *Proceedings of the Academy of Political Science*, May, 1963.

Assistance Act of 1963 where emphasis on the unwillingness of others to do their share was coupled with displeasure at divergent interpretations of the meaning of security obligations and spiced by charges of ingratitude for earlier favors rendered. Thus Senator Fulbright, traditionally a strong supporter of the foreign aid program, admitted that

ever since January 14 I have been troubled very much myself with the basic validity of this program under the present conditions.

That does not mean that I think it was not warranted in the beginning—the Turkish aid and the Marshall plan—but the developments in Western Europe under the leadership of France have not been reassuring at all.[1]

And Senator Fulbright asked whether "the very largest recipient of aid since the whole program began, including the Marshall Plan, was France, was it not?"[2] The colloquy following this question illuminates some of the difficulties the aid program now encounters.

MR. BELL. Yes, sir, that is correct, counting military and economic aid together over $9 billion.

THE CHAIRMAN. Won't you agree that our experience with France is somewhat disillusioning since the 14th of January?

MR. BELL. They have certainly followed policies, Mr. Chairman, that we do not agree with. [Deleted].

THE CHAIRMAN. I agree with that.

MR. BELL. On the other hand, sir, may I say, as I understand, the basic purpose for an assistance program has been and is to assist other countries to establish themselves as independent and self-supporting nations.

And no one can doubt that, with Marshall Plan aid, France has become an independent and self-supporting nation.

[1] *Foreign Assistance Act of 1963*, Hearings before the Committee on Foreign Relations, United States Senate, 88th Cong., 1st sess., p. 5.
[2] Same, p. 84.

The principal AID reply to Congressional charges that others are not doing enough is to point to increasing contributions from countries formerly receiving U.S. assistance. "The United States is not alone in providing capital and technical assistance. Because of the success of past aid programs in Europe and Japan, these nations now provide more than 40 percent of the total economic aid to less-developed countries."[3]

And Secretary McNamara called attention to the fact that in recent years a number of NATO countries have been increasing their contribution to their own defense.

Denmark has raised theirs 30 percent in the last 2 years, Germany 40 percent, Italy 22 percent, Norway 28 percent.

Secondly, that they are making these increases at a time when their gross national product per capita in many cases is substantially less than half of ours, and in practically no case is it more than half of ours.[4]

An examination of Congressional hearings and debate in recent years on the foreign aid program suggests certain conclusions regarding the attitudes of the principal Congressional defenders of the program. They tend to regard foreign economic assistance as an integral part of mutual security policy, deriving its main justification from such contribution as it is able to make to this policy. The question of equitable burden-sharing in their eyes relates not only to the cost of economic development assistance, but also to overseas military assistance and to domestic defense expenditures. Equitable participation, moreover, means to them a sharing of a conception of the means relevant to the pursuit of mutual security as well as a sharing of the costs. No one can complain of the size of the French contribution. French defense expenditures, as a per cent of national income, are among the heaviest in Western Europe. And France's public contribution to overseas economic development represents a substantially larger share of national income than ours. The complaint is that France

3 Same, p. 68.
4 Same, p. 212.

has divergent views on the uses to which these expenditures should be put.

Despite these differences we continue to have mutual interests not only with countries receiving aid but also with our allies in Western Europe and elsewhere who participate in the North Atlantic Treaty Organization and the Organization for Economic Cooperation and Development. But though these interests are mutual, they are not identical; and it is the diversity rather than the mutuality of interests that complicates the problem of burden-sharing. The Clay Committee was much exercised by this problem, and certain of its recommendations concerning the geographical distribution of American aid are in recognition of a diversity of interests vis-à-vis our European allies. The Committee, for example, recommended that in those areas in Africa in which European countries have strong continuing interests the United States should encourage its European allies to carry the major share of the aid burden. Continuing interest is evidenced by the persistence of a pattern of trade and investment, by the presence in these areas of European businessmen and civil servants engaged in technical assistance, and by the willingness of the metropoles to dispense sizable quantities of aid. French assistance to countries in the franc zone of Northwest Africa is large, and the United Kingdom has assumed sizable commitments in its former colonies in East and West Africa.[5]

To a certain extent this sharing of the burden along geographical lines accentuates the diversity rather than the mutuality of interest between the United States and its Western European allies. Futhermore, the receiving countries normally would prefer to obtain assistance from several sources rather than be excessively dependent on one. Pushed to its logical limits, a geographical sharing of the aid burden would tend to perpetuate

[5] This view is apparently accepted by AID. "The allocation of AID funds recognizes the special interests of the United States in Latin America, where we furnish three-quarters of the total aid, and of the European countries in Africa, where foreign aid is predominantly European." Statement of David E. Bell, cited, p. 69.

existing spheres of influence and perhaps create others that had not existed before. To strengthen a mutuality of interest, the ideal solution would appear to be a sharing of the aid burden on a world-wide basis with all aid dispensers participating in all areas in proportion to their relative capacities. But there are other difficulties, apart from historic ties, that militate against this solution. Japanese and German reparation payments are usually considered to be part of aid, and, of necessity, this flow is directed toward particular countries. For some countries the willingness to supply aid undoubtedly springs mainly from the desire to establish trade connections, and these seem more promising in certain areas than in others. The shipment of P.L. 480 surpluses naturally goes to those countries able to absorb this type of import. As we saw in the last chapter, what is usually called aid includes a very mixed bag indeed, and there are real difficulties entirely apart from the influence of historic connections in attaining equitable burden-sharing on a world-wide basis.

There will be many who see in the recommendations of the Clay Committee, and the policies now followed by AID both an additional recognition of the disarray into which our Western alliance is tending to fall and some insensitivity to the natural desire of underdeveloped countries to escape from excessive dependence on their former colonial masters. There may be some truth in both these allegations. On the other hand, both the Clay Committee and the administration recognize that there are a number of African countries where our interests are not likely to be served by a predominant reliance on European assistance. In these countries the United States must play a major role. Nigeria is one of them. Secondly, the United States continues to press in O.E.C.D. and elsewhere, and with some success, for increased European participation in foreign aid in various parts of the world. Finally, it may be well to recognize that there *is* a diversity as well as a mutuality of interest in foreign aid and that this diversity is likely to persist.

Burden-sharing, as suggested above, embraces a much wider collection of interests than foreign aid. The first postwar exercise in burden-sharing was concerned primarily with appropriate defense expenditures within the framework of NATO and had nothing to do with foreign aid to underdeveloped countries. It would be convenient if we could separate the sharing of the foreign aid burden from other types of burden-sharing, but this is difficult for at least two reasons. The relations between the Atlantic allies are such that what a country does in one sphere of burden-sharing affects its ability and disposition to share burdens in others. And it also affects the tactics used by the United States or by other countries in attempting to secure a more equitable sharing of the aid burden. Currently, for example, the United States is a sizable supplier of military assistance to Greece and Turkey. On the surface it might appear desirable to attempt to persuade our allies to accept a share of this burden. But it might be even more desirable to induce them to increase their domestic military expenditures, say for conventional forces, or to provide a larger measure of economic assistance to Southern Asia. What they can be persuaded to do in one direction is likely to affect their willingness to act in others. Consequently the sharing of the foreign aid burden tends to become interrelated with other aspects of the total mutual security problem.

Secondly, as I suggested in Chapter 2, the foreign aid policies of various countries have certain relations with their trade policies. A trade policy in Western Europe designed to permit an increase in the export earnings of underdeveloped areas may do more to assist economic development than a considerable volume of foreign aid, and, under certain circumstances, it may be more feasible to put into effect. Consequently the question of how much foreign aid a country is willing to undertake tends to be affected by what it is doing in the field of trade policy and by what is being done to it by the trade policies of others. I want to return presently to the relation of aid and trade as it affects the problem of burden-sharing, but at this point we need to say a word about the character of "burdens" and the meaning of equitable sharing.

꿗꿗꿗

Is it a burden if I am asked to pay $10 for an article I want which customarily sells for $10 in the market? The answer presumably is "No." I am free to choose whether to buy it or not; and if I do decide to buy, it is because at that particular time and place the article seems worth more to me than $10. Consequently, parting with $10 is no burden. Contrast this, however, with the situation in which I am asked to part with a few thousand dollars in income taxes for which I receive in return a not very easily defined bundle of government services. There is no doubt that paying taxes is regarded as a burden. Indeed, the poor citizen groaning under the tax burden is a favorite theme for cartoonists and writers of editorials.

It is easy to specify the reason why paying taxes is considered burdensome while parting with money in the market is not. First, there is the element of compulsion. Second, there is the difficulty of comparing value received with value given up. Third, there is the realization that the services of government, whatever they are judged to be worth, are likely to be available to me whether I pay my taxes or not. In the market place, the rule is "No tickee, no shirtee." But in this other realm, evasion or avoidance of taxation, if it is possible, does not necessarily mean a diminution of services received—an important consideration in burden-sharing.

When we move from the individual purchaser or taxpayer to his government viewed as a dispenser of foreign aid, to what extent and under what circumstances must we consider foreign aid to be a burden? In order to consider this problem at all, we have to envisage government as an entity making choices which affect the interests of the nation as a whole. If the objective of foreign aid is simply and exclusively the security of the United States, one can ask the question, as of any purchase, whether we are receiving fair value; but, assuming we are, it is difficult to see that any burden is involved. If, as the Clay Committee suggests, our military aid expenditures dollar for dollar contribute more to our security than corresponding expenditures in our defense appropriations, it is hard to see that a "burden" is involved. There is certainly a burden for the taxpayer as there is in the funding of any type of public expenditure, but from the point of view of the government as representative of the national interest, "burden" may be an inappropriate term.

Suppose, however, that we consider aid to be a disinterested contribution from wealthy countries to promote the economic development of poorer ones. There are many who think this either is, or should be, the primary purpose of aid. The two eminent European economists mentioned in Chapter 2, Gunnar Myrdal and Jan Tinbergen, envision aid as a twentieth-century extension in the international sphere of those principles of the welfare state that the last hundred years has witnessed in the domestic sphere. There is no doubt that under these circumstances aid would be considered to be a burden. Perhaps it shouldn't be, but we have not yet reached that stage—if we ever do—where the needs of one's neighbors are given the same priority as one's own needs. Any transfer of resources from one country to another without an equivalent *quid pro quo* is commonly considered to be burdensome. The more we receive—or can be made to appear to receive—for our money, the less burdensome the outlay.

The foregoing argument would seem to indicate either that the term "burden" is inappropriately used in connection with foreign aid expenditures or that considerable doubt exists whether in fact we do receive an adequate *quid pro quo* for these expenditures. That the latter consideration is controlling is suggested by the difference in Congressional attitude toward domestic defense expenditures, foreign military assistance, and foreign economic assistance. Defense expenditures are customarily voted with a readiness that implies that, in this area, we know we are getting something for our money. Military assistance is less effectively supported, but Congress in general is willing to go along with a military judgment that such assistance contributes to U.S. security. It is primarily in the area of overseas economic assistance that serious doubts arise. And these doubts tend to be reinforced by a conviction that we are doing more than "our share."

This brings us to the question of equitable sharing. Everyone agrees that taxes are burdensome, and a great deal of attention has been paid to the issue of equity in taxation. It would have to be said that the literature on this subject has not got much beyond the general proposition that those in similar economic situations should bear similar tax burdens. Considerable difficulties are encountered in determining when in fact situations are similar. Much greater difficulties are encountered in determining what treatment is equitable when situations are dissimilar. The state cuts through these difficulties by the imposition of its authority. It is left to government to determine the level and direction of public spending and to assess the burden equitably among the various taxable units. In a democratic society it can probably be said that the outcome of these decisions represents a rough consensus of majority opinion. But for those who disagree there is no recourse except through the ballot box. If it were left to the taxpayers to agree on equitable sharing by open discussion, it is doubtful whether tax payments would be large.

This is, however, the only way in which the equitable sharing of the aid burden can be achieved. There is no overriding authority to bring the discussion to a halt and assess contributions, though there are various carrots and sticks that can be and are put to use. If there is to be even a modicum of success in the burden-sharing exercise, two conditions need to be fulfilled. First, there must be some mutuality of interest, some recognition of common purpose among the potential contributors. Second, there must be at least a rough consensus concerning the meaning of equitable sharing. Does this imply equal per capita contributions; does it mean equal percentage shares of national income? Should there be an element of progression in the assessment; should certain countries with low per capita income be exempt? Despite some progress, neither one of these conditions has been adequately attained in the burden-sharing operations to date.

As I pointed out in Chapter 1, discussions of burden-sharing are also plagued by differences of opinion on the meaning of foreign aid. The Development Assistance Committee found it impossible to arrive at a definition with which its members could agree, and now contents itself with reporting the annual flow of long-term financial resources to developing countries and multi-lateral agencies. In effect this means that any financial transfer with a maturity of five years or more is considered to partake of the nature of aid. If we look at changes in this flow over the last few years, the figures seem to indicate a rather satisfactory increase. The total transfer increased from about $7½ billion in 1960 to nearly $8¾ billion in 1961. Most of this increase was in the form of public grants and loans which mounted to nearly $6 billion in 1961. Any optimism that might be generated by these figures is, however, somewhat illusory. The over-all data for 1962 show no perceptible change in the flow of public funds. Foreign private investment declined by about $200 million. Furthermore, certain transfers that are called foreign aid will inevitably decline. In 1961 financial transfers included $133 million in reparation payments, principally from Germany and Japan. The current figures are also somewhat inflated as the result of commitments of the United Kingdom to former colonies in Africa; these are for a limited period. It is therefore not at all clear that the total flow of long-term resources from the developed countries is definitely on the increase.

There is another side of the picture that in certain respects is even more serious. In some underdeveloped countries which are large foreign aid recipients, the ability to service foreign loans on anything like commercial terms is rapidly approaching a limit. Foreign service charges now amount to 17 per cent of India's total foreign exchange earnings and is likely to increase to around 30 per cent in the next five to ten years. The situation in some other countries is as bad or worse. If aid cannot be provided on softer terms, the transfer of financial resources to these countries, because of difficulties of repayment, is likely to decline rather than increase. Although there has been a substantial lengthening of maturities and some decrease in interest rates over the last few years, there is still a large gap between the terms on which the United States is willing to provide resources and those of most of the other foreign aid suppliers. France is the only country whose average terms approach those of the United States. In the burden-sharing exercise, terms and conditions relating to financial transfers are at least as important as total quantities.

So much for aid in the form of financial transfers. In a broader sense, however, aid encompasses more than this. The economic development of poor countries is facilitated by adding to their resources, particularly in the form of scarce foreign exchange. Anything that the rich countries do to augment these resources has some claim to be considered aid. Or, if we reject this extension of the meaning of aid and insist on a sharp distinction between trade and aid, we should recognize that policy changes in the rich countries designed to enable poor countries to increase their trade earnings have some of the elements of burden-sharing. Impediments to imports into the industrialized countries of food and raw materials from the underdeveloped world obviously lessen foreign exchange earnings. Furthermore, if poor countries are to escape from exclusive dependence on raw materials exports, they must diversify, and diversification will be greatly facilitated by the willingness of the advanced countries to move over and yield part of their domestic market for light manufactures.

A reduction of trade barriers by the advanced countries does not, strictly speaking, mean that a burden is assumed. In the long run it presumably means a shift of resources from less efficient to more efficient lines of production. New England, in losing its textile industry, has transferred resources to the field of electronics which is more profitable and more closely adapted to the comparative advantages of the region. In the long run this is likely to be true of countries willing to share their domestic markets with imports from underdeveloped countries. But the short-run effects of this process on employment and profits are apt to appear as distinctly burdensome. And it is unlikely that there can be marked reductions in barriers to imports from poor countries without some concerted action on the part of the advanced countries to share this "burden."

The United States restricts imports of copper, lead, zinc, oil, and other important earners of foreign exchange for under-developed countries. Western Europe imposes restraints on imports of tropical products or limits the domestic consumption of these products by high excise taxes. Almost all of the advanced countries have systems of taxation favoring the processing of imported materials by their own nationals as against processing in the country of origin. If significant steps are to be taken by advanced countries to permit the increase of trade earnings in poor countries, it will probably require concerted action. In fact, in the so-called "Kennedy round" of tariff negotiations between the United States and the European Common Market, provision is made for a discussion of a joint reduction of tariffs on exports from less developed countries. There is a certain measure of agreement that such reduction should be made without a requirement that the less developed countries make reciprocal concessions. But it is extremely unlikely that such a step would be taken except in concert. This is apt to appear to the advanced countries as an exercise in burden-sharing.

The characteristics of a burden are more clearly evident in proposals to increase the foreign exchange earnings of raw materials exporters through various types of commodity agreements. It is pointed out that the terms of trade for raw material exporters have significantly worsened since 1952. And it is further calculated that a fall of only ten per cent in the average price of exports from the underdeveloped world can cancel the whole effect of aid rendered by financial transfers. If foreign exchange earnings are to be bolstered by commodity agreements fixing the price of exports at an average level higher than would be attained on the free market, there is no doubt that the importing countries are assuming a burden. It is not a tax burden imposed by the governments of the importing countries, but a burden borne by the consumers of the products in question and shared, as among countries, in proportion to their imports of commodities under agreement. It is a complicated question whether this is the best way to render aid to the underdeveloped world, but there is no question that this is aid rather than trade.

If we are to carry the analysis of burden-sharing this far, we might as well go one step further. Not only the burden itself but ability to carry the burden is affected by the nature of permissible trade patterns. Japan's contribution to aid through financial transfers is almost exclusively limited to reparations and capital lending at close to commercial rates. The Japanese complain, and with reason, that their contribution cannot be more generous because of balance-of-payments limitations imposed by restrictions in Western Europe and the United States against imports from Japan. If these restrictions were softened, Japan's ability to bear a larger aid burden would be increased. In a recent report to the Senate it is pointed out that Western European countries have fewer inhibitions than we do toward trading with Eastern Europe.[6] They thus improve their balance-of-payments position and hence their ability to bear the aid burdens. The report goes on to suggest the desirability of equalizing the commercial opportunities for American exporters, particularly of agricultural commodities, by lowering the legislative and executive restrictions on U.S. exports to Iron Curtain countries.

We have perhaps said enough to indicate that sharing the burden of aid embraces a complex set of problems involving not only the amounts, terms, and conditions of financial transfer, but also existing and possible patterns of international trade as they affect the export earnings of underdeveloped countries and the capacity of advanced countries to make an aid contribution. Having broadened the concept so extensively, I now propose to narrow it and concentrate the remainder of this chapter on the issues that have recently formed the center of the debate.

[6] U.S. Congress, Senate Committee on Foreign Relations, *Berlin in a Changing Europe*, Report of Mike Mansfield, J. Caleb Boggs, Claiborne Pell, and Benjamin S. Smith, January 22, 1963. Recent sales of U.S. wheat to the Soviet Union and of corn to Hungary suggest that U.S. policy with respect to trade with Eastern Europe is in process of change.

𝄢𝄢𝄢

As SUGGESTED above, the three areas in which debate on burden-sharing have been most intensive are defense expenditures within the framework of NATO, military assistance to poorer countries both inside and outside of NATO, and economic development assistance to the underdeveloped world. Sharing the burden of defense expenditures within NATO is primarily a question of the appropriate diversion of domestic resources to military purposes, and financial transfers among countries are not involved to any considerable extent. Military and economic development assistance do involve intercountry transfers, and I am discussing aid here only in terms of such transfers without going into the question of changes in trade patterns.

To speak very generally, and assume a solution of the problem of equitable sharing in terms of a fixed percentage of national income, the United States bears far more than its share of total NATO expenditures, is almost the sole contributor to military assistance (at least since the French have withdrawn from Algeria), and bears something like an equitable share of economic development assistance.

U.S. defense expenditures are between three and four times the total expenditures of all the other NATO countries taken together. In addition, the United States is the only NATO country apart from Greece and Turkey that maintains a twenty-four month period for its national service conscripts. In the other NATO countries, this varies from zero, as in Great Britain, to eighteen months, as in France. Given a situation in which it is widely conceded that the defense of Western Europe and the United States is indivisible, why is there this discrepancy in willingness to contribute?

There seem to be several reasons, some good and some bad. There is first a disposition to question a concept of equitable sharing that runs in terms of a fixed percentage of national income and to insist on various degrees of progression. Even in the industrialized countries of NATO, per capita incomes in 1961

ranged from $700 in Italy to $2,900 in the United States. With due
allowances for differences in purchasing power of the various cur-
rencies at prevailing exchange rates, there still is a great variation
in per capita real incomes. Secondly, there is a disposition to
question the appropriate level of NATO defense expenditures.
Without doubt there is a feeling that defense expenditures in the
United States are somewhat out of hand. Then there is an inevitable resentment against the facts of life that assign priority
in nuclear expenditures to the United States and priority in conventional forces to Western Europe. But after all these and other
considerations are taken into account, there remains the problem
that bedevils any kind of burden-sharing by mutual agreement.
This is the realization that there is no very close connection
between the size of the contribution and what is received in
exchange. The United States is not going to reduce its defense
expenditures because all or a few other countries do not do their
part. It is difficult to resist the conclusion that certain countries
are enjoying a more or less free ride and that they are well content
with this position.

It is impossible to draw a sharp distinction between military
and economic development assistance, and I shall not attempt to
do so. In fiscal year 1963 appropriations under the U.S. Military
Assistance Program amounted to $1,375 million and appropria-
tions for the Agency for International Development to $2,525
million, exclusive of P.L. 480 expenditures, Export-Import Bank
loans, or outlays for the Peace Corps. No data are known to me
that permit a precise estimate of the contribution of other countries to military assistance, but there is no doubt that the amounts
are small. The United Kingdom has recently and generously
agreed to share the burden of military assistance to India, and
some small part of other countries' aid contributions is devoted
to military expenditures. But the United States carries the lion's
share of the military assistance program, and it is unlikely to be
able to shift this burden in any considerable measure to other
shoulders. On the whole it appears easier to persuade our European allies to increase their own defense expenditures than to

contribute to military assistance to others. Security may be a mutual affair, but the element of mutuality appears to thin out perceptibly as the area of expenditure moves away from the domestic hearth. American military assistance is concentrated in nine countries, all on the periphery of the Communist world; and if the defense of these countries is considered essential to the security of the free world, we are likely to continue to be the only significant providers of military assistance.

The situation is quite different in the field of economic development assistance. In 1961, 86 per cent of all economic assistance was bilateral. Of the bilateral assistance from the free world, 98 per cent came from countries belonging to the Development Assistance Committee plus Australia and New Zealand. All these countries have some form of aid agency, all have some technical cooperation program, and all finance capital projects. The public flow of development funds from countries in this group other than the United States was about as high a percentage of their total gross national product as was that from the United States. Furthermore, many European countries have gone rather far during the last few years in softening the terms of their loans.

Reflection on the rather different attitude of our Western European allies toward sharing the burdens of defense expenditures of the Atlantic area, of military assistance to overseas countries, and of economic development assistance, may throw some light on the procedures that may be effective in bringing about some redistribution of the burden. If I may characterize these attitudes in terms that are admittedly too sweeping, they appear to be about as follows: the obligation to contribute to the defense of the Atlantic community is recognized by all, and, despite recent eruptions of a somewhat antique brand of nationalism, I would expect these obligations to continue to be recognized. There will be differences of opinion on the appropriate level of defense expenditures and on how they should be shared. On these and other matters we must expect to see European powers given greater weight in the process of decision-making, and, as they are, we may also expect to see them assume a greater share of the burden. As suggested above, there is already substantial evidence that this is in train.

On the other hand, the obligation to contribute to military assistance to countries outside the NATO framework is recognized to only a limited extent, and I see no reason to expect that this attitude will change.

Other countries do make token contributions to military assistance in Korea and Viet-Nam. The United Kingdom, as we have mentioned, has been willing to assume an equal share of initial military assistance to India. But around the Sino-Soviet periphery from Greece and Turkey to Korea the United States is by far the predominant contributor. There are some advantages in funneling equipment and logistical support from a single source rather than dividing responsibility among many. But presumably the principal reason for not pushing harder for a more equitable sharing of this particular burden is a judgment that it is somewhat easier to obtain results in the area of domestic defense expenditures and foreign economic assistance. Total military assistance is a relatively small item as compared to the total defense expenditures, and in certain parts of the world we are not, in any case, interested in sharing this particular burden. I have already pointed out that a number of NATO countries have in fact substantially increased their defense expenditures in recent years. And there has been a considerable increase in the willingness of other countries to contribute to economic development assistance programs.

In this country, as we have seen, there is a disposition to think of all three "burden-sharing" areas as intimately related. All tend to be treated as essential parts of the one overriding problem of assuring the security of the free world. If defense expenditures, military assistance, and economic development assistance are all necessary to strengthen the security of the free world, why shouldn't other countries contribute in such fashion as to make possible an equitable sharing of the total burden? In fact, whether rightly or wrongly, the problem is not so regarded outside the United States. With respect to economic development assistance in particular, other countries contribute for a mixture of reasons, in which mixture security considerations may not be very important.

What seems to be important, among other reasons accounting for the flow of grants and long-term loans to underdeveloped areas, are considerations of national prestige, trade interests, and, by no means least, a rather disinterested desire to promote the economic development of these areas. Of course, there should be mentioned in addition the desire of the United States to get rid of surplus agricultural output, some continuing flow of reparations payments, particularly from Japan, and remaining obligations, recognized particularly by the United Kingdom, to give for a period a financial helping hand to former colonies. Reparations and ex-colonial obligations are a dwindling source of assistance. On the other hand not only is P.L. 480 apparently here to stay, but agricultural surpluses from Western Europe may well, in a few years, join those from the United States. In any case it is clear that, apart from the United States and France (though on the basis of a different conception), security interests are not a very important explanation of the flow of funds to underdeveloped areas. This needs to be taken into account by the United States in any attempt to bring about a redistribution of the burden.

Let me say, in conclusion, a few words about recent attempts of this country to bring about such a redistribution of the economic development assistance burden. These attempts have largely focused on the Development Assistance Committee of the Organization for Economic Cooperation and Development, on the various consortia and consultative groups brought together to help finance the programs of particular countries, and on those U.N. agencies primarily concerned with development problems.

Discussions of "burden-sharing" have been a staple fare of the Development Assistance Committee ever since its beginning. A Resolution of March 1961, accepted by all member governments, recommends that "Members agree to expand the flow of resources to the less-developed countries, to improve the effectiveness of development assistance, and to provide for increased

assistance in the form of grants or loans on favorable terms."
During 1962 the organization established an annual aid review
in which the members submit for each other's scrutiny and
criticism a record of their development assistance efforts during
the previous year. These efforts have not been without effect. The
flow of financial resources from D.A.C. governments to developing countries and multilateral agencies increased from $4,895
million in 1960 to $5,953 million in 1961 although, as I have
pointed out, this rate of increase is unlikely to continue. And in
recent years there has been some improvement from the point of
view of the developing countries in the terms on which these
resources have been made available.

A second forum for the discussion of burden-sharing has been
provided by various consortia and consultative groups. Here the
United States has frequently attempted a matching procedure.
This has been particularly conspicuous in the consortia organized
to finance the Indian and the Pakistani development plans. The
matching procedure has had some effect in increasing the contribution of other countries but probably at the expense of
hardening the terms on which new money has become available.
Indeed the American participants have felt at times that the U.S.
contributions in long-term, low interest-bearing loans would inevitably come to be used to pay off the short-term high interest-
bearing contributions of other participants.

A serious defect of the matching procedure is that it deprives
the receiving country of much of the incentive to negotiate for
better terms. If, for example, Japan offers as part of its matching
contribution to the Indian consortium $10 million repayable in
ten years at six per cent, the Indian government may find itself
unable to refuse the Japanese contribution without losing an
equivalent amount of U.S. money at three-quarters per cent
interest repayable in forty years. It may well be that both the
United States and the country receiving assistance would benefit
from a less rigorous insistence on matching, with more freedom
for the receiving country to negotiate better terms. In fact, U.S.
policy seems to be shifting in this direction.

Finally, the United States, to the extent it can make use of United Nations agencies to promote development, enjoys an automatic burden-sharing device in the shape of the contribution percentages fixed for U.N. members; provided, of course, that the United Nations can enforce its assessments. The U.S. quota is normally in the neighborhood of 30 per cent, although in the International Development Association it is 42 per cent. There are certain areas in which the objectives of the U.S. Aid Program can be as effectively—or even more effectively—attained through an international agency than by means of a straight bilateral arrangement. This is particularly true in the area in which I.D.A. normally operates. In view of its established record as an effective development agency and the automatic burden-sharing provisions which its charter provides, it is somewhat surprising that the American government has not until recently pressed harder to supplement I.D.A.'s dwindling supply of development funds. I.D.A. capital has now been replenished to the extent of $750 million, and a majority of the Senate Foreign Relations Committee apparently favors a large-scale transfer of development financing from the Development Loan Fund to the International Development Association. It may be surmised, however, that the real limitation to expansion of I.D.A. resources will turn out to be the unwillingness of various European governments to match the U.S. contributions on the present I.D.A. burden-sharing terms.

Perhaps I have said enough to suggest that the equitable sharing of military and economic aid burdens is a subject embracing an extremely complicated set of problems. They are unlikely to be amenable to tidy solution in the absence of very close agreement among the countries of the Atlantic Community on such matters as military strategy, the appropriate levels of defense spending, the purpose of economic assistance, the relation between trade and aid, and what constitutes "equity" in burden-sharing. Although we are very far from close agreement on many of the matters, enough progress has been made to justify, perhaps a modest degree of optimism.

4
THE ALLIANCE
FOR PROGRESS

THE PRECEDING chapters have not attempted to emphasize the regional differences among countries in the underdeveloped world, though these obviously have an important bearing on the process of economic and political development and on the character of foreign aid as an instrument of U.S. foreign policy. Latin America, however, has a special set of economic and political relations with the United States that has recently been recognized by the establishment of the Alliance for Progress. The Alliance is the first attempt since the Marshall Plan to introduce regional organization into the administration of foreign aid, and the differences and similarities between the Marshall Plan and the Alliance will concern us later in this chapter.

The U.S. trade and investment relationships with Latin America are, of course, closer and more significant than with any other less developed area. Approximately 50 per cent of Latin American exports flow to the United States, and approximately 50 per cent of Latin American imports come from the United States. For Mexico, Colombia, and Guatemala the figures are closer to 75 per cent. It is only in Argentina and Uruguay that trade is more closely tied to Western Europe. For Latin America as a whole, roughly 95 per cent of exports take the form of agricultural products, minerals, and fuels. The percentages vary from 99 per cent in Colombia and Bolivia, to 92 per cent in Brazil. Since the prices of many of these exports are highly volatile and since, after 1952, the terms of trade have tended to run rather strongly against Latin American exports, an interest of long standing in the instrumentalities for stabilizing and raising the price of raw material exports has been reinforced. Any consideration of aid for Latin America tends to become involved with trade policies. And since the United States is by far the largest market for Latin American exports, it is American trade policies that are of primary concern.

By 1962 U.S. private investment in Latin America was in excess of $12 billion, which is a multiple of the total of U.S. private investment in the remainder of the less developed world. Traditionally, this investment has flowed into minerals and fuels and, until recently, into public utilities, but since World War II there has been a substantial investment in manufacturing, particularly in Brazil and Mexico. Recently, however, the flow of U.S. private direct investment on a net basis into Latin America has all but ceased. From $618 million in 1956, and $1,163 million in 1957, net direct U.S. private investment declined to $141 million in 1961 and a negative $32 million in 1962.[1] These figures are, of course, misleading as indicators of the current contribution of foreign private investment to Latin American productivity and development. They do not take into account either the very large reinvestment by American firms in Latin America of earnings and depreciation allowances or the attendant flows of new techniques and managerial competence. Nevertheless, both the size of the U.S. investment stake in Latin America and the recent lessening of external additions to this stake, suggest aspects of Latin American development, and of the U.S. interest in this development, that are intimately related to foreign aid policy. The ques-

----

[1] These figures are heavily influenced by variations in petroleum investment. In 1962, the net outflow of capital to Latin America by various categories was as follows:

Mining and smelting	− $3 million
Petroleum	−115
Manufacturing	114
Other	− 28
Total	−$32 million

Survey of Current Business, August, 1963. p. 18.

tion of the appropriate role of private investment in the foreign aid program is particularly significant and relevant for Latin America.

The special political interests of the United States in Latin America have been manifest since the announcement of the Monroe Doctrine in 1823. This was a unilateral declaration, unenforceable during the nineteenth century except for the benign assistance of the British navy. Nevertheless, though unilateral, it was welcomed by the newly independent Latin American republics and enshrined more than a century later as an inter-American doctrine in the Act of Chapultepec in 1945 and the Reciprocal Assistance Treaty of 1947. In the interval, more active, rather than purely defensive, interests of the United States in Latin America had been made evident by the acquisition of territory from Mexico, the promotion of the Panamanian revolt against Colombia, the several armed interventions in Central America and the Caribbean during the administration of the first Roosevelt, and in Mexico during the early years of the Wilson administration. After World War I, under the astute ministrations of Ambassador Dwight Morrow, the United States made its peace with Mexico and this effort, well begun, blossomed in the 1930s into the Good Neighbor Policy. The policy carried the strong implication of nonintervention, at least unilaterally, in Latin America; and despite the action in Guatemala in 1954 and the abortive Cuban incident in 1961, it would appear to be established policy that the United States is no longer likely to intervene in Latin American affairs except in concert with its fellow members of the Organization of American States. The Organization is the outgrowth of a long series of inter-American conferences beginning in 1890, and, though relatively weak, is one of the indications of the special regional characteristics of U.S. relations with Latin America.

This long but chequered, hot-cold relationship between the United States and Latin America must be borne in mind in considering the problems now faced by the Alliance for Progress. There *is* a strong consciousness of common security interests

among the American States, but the history of U.S. intervention—
some of it fairly recent—suggests to Latin America that the
United States is perhaps too prone to substitute its own interpretation of these interests for the common judgment. Latin
America *is* more closely tied by trade relationships to the United
States than to any other part of the world, but this is apt to be
felt as dependence rather than common economic interest. The
overwhelming predominance of the United States as a military
and economic power is not conducive to an easy relationship
among members of the Organization of American States. Nor has
the history of our foreign aid activities prior to the formation of
the Alliance for Progress given much comfort to Latin America.

Until recently it has been assumed in the United States that
trade and foreign private investment were the appropriate sources
of foreign exchange for Latin American economic development.
Apart from relatively small technical assistance programs, public
financial assistance has been pretty much limited to loans from
the Export-Import Bank and International Bank at close to commercial terms. This has, of course, contrasted strongly with the
treatment by U.S. foreign aid agencies of other parts of the world.
Immediately after the war, the United States furnished some $14
billion in economic assistance to Western Europe on a purely
grant basis. After the Marshall Plan, Asia and the Middle East
became the favored areas, later to be followed by Africa, with
grants and soft loans the preferred media of assistance. Finally, it
would have to be said that not since Sumner Welles occupied the
position of Under Secretary of State has there been an American
government official in a top policy-making position whose primary interests have been in Latin America.

Beginning in 1958, a series of steps have brought about pro-
found changes in U.S. policy toward economic relations with
Latin America. In that year President Kubitschek of Brazil published his proposal for Operation Pan America concerned with
the collective responsibility for economic development in Latin
America, and the United States agreed to the establishment of
an Inter-American Development Bank. In 1960 President Eisen-

hower promised financial assistance for social development programs in Latin America, and the Act of Bogotá was signed committing the Latin American countries to a series of institutional reforms and the United States to financial assistance. This was followed in the early months of the Kennedy administration by the launching of the Alliance for Progress. All this represents an almost revolutionary change, but Latin Americans may, perhaps, be forgiven for thinking it a somewhat belated response accelerated by the security shocks connected with the treatment of Vice President Nixon in Peru and Venezuela in 1958 and by the Cuban revolution in 1959. The deductions drawn therefrom concerning appropriate ways of inducing American foreign aid generosity have plagued the first two years of the Alliance for Progress and still represent a problem to be managed.

IN MANY ways, the task of assisting economic development in Latin America is much simpler than in other parts of the world. Indeed, the leading countries can hardly be called underdeveloped. Of the seven largest states accounting for 85 per cent of the population (Argentina, Brazil, Chile, Colombia, Mexico, Peru, and Venezuela), only Peru has a per capita income of less than $200. In Venezuela per capita incomes approach $700. This contrasts with $75 in India, $65 in Pakistan, and the $50-$100 per capita incomes characteristic of most of sub-Saharan Africa. Although population is growing rapidly, there is no over-all shortage of arable land. Latin America has, in potentially arable acreage, about three and a half times as much per capita as the average for the world as a whole. With the exception of coal, it is rich in mineral resources. The literacy rate is higher, on the average, than in other large areas of the underdeveloped world, and in a number of countries there has emerged a sizable group of vigorous entrepreneurs.

It would appear that in most of the larger Latin American countries plus Uruguay, the basic conditions of economic growth are present. Indeed, all these countries have, at one time or another, experienced rapid economic development, and in Brazil, Mexico and Venezuela the process is continuing. Yet, even in these countries, with the possible exception of Mexico, the prospects would have to be described as precarious. In Argentina and Chile per capita incomes have actually declined over the last decade. In Peru and Colombia development has been an off-and-on affair with periods of expansion alternating with periods of stagnation. When one proceeds, moreover, from these rather favorably situated countries to Bolivia, Ecuador, Paraguay, some of the Central America republics, and to Haiti, one is clearly back in the underdeveloped world, with per capita incomes ranging from $90 in Haiti and Bolivia to $300 in Costa Rica. Furthermore, even in the relatively advanced countries there are large areas of extreme poverty. The huge northeast area of Brazil has a per capita income of only $140 as compared to approximately $300 for Brazil as a whole and close to $500 for the south. Rio de Janeiro and Lima are notable for their extensive slum areas. And the Indian populations of the Andean republics and of western Brazil are among the most poverty-stricken in the world.

The contrast between the progressive and the traditional and between rich and poor in Latin America is more striking than almost anywhere else in the underdeveloped world. These differences underlie some of the most recalcitrant obstacles to economic development in Latin America and to the success of the Alliance for Progress. From a narrow economic point of view it might be said that the "inputs" of critical importance to Latin American development are foreign exchange and managerial capacity. These are, indeed, critical inputs, but if Latin American states possessed governments sufficiently well organized and sufficiently supported to be able to enact and to put into effect appropriate policies, these difficulties could, with some assistance from abroad, be overcome. The fundamental obstacles to economic development are political. As I have suggested above, the promotion of economic development in Latin America appears in some respects to be relatively simple. If all that was needed, as in Western Europe under the Marshall Plan, was an influx for a limited period of time of sizable quantities of foreign exchange, it would indeed be simple. Unfortunately, there is more to the problem than that.

To say that the fundamental obstacles to economic development in Latin America are political is not to deny that such economic factors as shortage of foreign exchange are of decisive importance. The dollar value of per capita imports into Latin America has declined steadily since 1950, a period during which rapid growth could have been possible only with expanding per capita imports. A part—perhaps the major part—of the decline in import capacity has been the result of forces lying outside of Latin American control. The demand for Latin American exports *has* been sluggish and the terms of trade distinctly adverse. But part of the difficulty—and a significant part—must be attributed to governmental action or inaction. The lessening of foreign private investment is primarily the result of an unfavorable domestic climate that could have been made distinctly more favorable by appropriate government action. Foreign exchange difficulties have been accentuated by a flight from a number of countries of domestic capital. Uncontrolled inflation and persistently overvalued exchange rates have hampered exports. Various Latin American governments have nationalized foreign-owned utilities and have on occasion assumed a compensation liability in foreign exchange that could only worsen the balance of payments. Perhaps this action, or failure to act, has been inevitable within the Latin American political environment. If so, it is only another way of saying that the obstacles to development are largely, if not primarily, noneconomic.

The adverse effect on economic development of governmental policies has been accentuated by weaknesses in public administration and in government organization. None of the Latin American countries has been able to develop a civil service remotely comparable to, say, the Indian civil service in efficiency and absence of corruption. Perhaps Mexico comes closest but, even here, there is a marked difference. In many Latin American governments there is no effective budgetary control over the operations of spending ministries or public corporations. The most egregious failures concern the operations of government railways and other utilities whose annual deficits frequently place an intolerable burden on the government budget. In the absence of budgetary control, it is difficult to see how a development program assigning a large role to the public sector can be effectively implemented.

These are some of the reasons why, despite growth rates more rapid than in most of the underdeveloped world and the presence of conditions distinctly favorable to further growth, Latin American development is frequently interrupted and usually precarious. They also help to explain why providing external assistance to development presents a rather different problem than in some other parts of the underdeveloped world. I emphasized in Chapter 2 a distinction between countries in which the provision of access to imports is a necessary and sufficient condition of growth and countries for which it is a necessary but not a sufficient condition. The Latin American countries, in the main, belong in the second category. This is explicitly recognized in the Alliance for Progress which purports to be a "partnership" in which the Latin American countries agree to undertake various steps to help themselves while the United States, in concert with other countries and international lending agencies, agrees to provide increased access to foreign exchange. Both conditions are necessary. But how to bring them about, how to yoke this pair of horses so that each pulls his appropriate weight, raises an extraordinarily difficult set of problems.

So far as the foreign aid policy of the United States is concerned, it raises in an acute form the question of the "strings" that may appropriately be attached to aid, briefly discussed in

Chapter 2. Aid to various Latin American countries is, or can be, peculiarly susceptible to misuse. Unless governments are willing to take measures designed to increase their own contributions to economic development and to make effective use of increased access to foreign exchange, aid may be wasted. Yet these measures may frequently be unpopular, and the position of many Latin American governments is sufficiently precarious to set fairly narrow limits to their potential scope of action. Under these circumstances, how much leverage does the instrument of foreign aid give us to induce necessary changes? And under what auspices? I shall return to these questions presently. But, first, it is necessary to consider the relation of trade and foreign investment to Latin American development and to the U.S. aid program.

✿✿✿

ALTHOUGH increased access to foreign exchange is not a sufficient condition for sustained growth in most Latin American countries, it is a highly important condition. In the public sector the capital requirements for necessary expansion of social overhead facilities —railways, roads, communications, electric power, port facilities, and the like—are high and the import content per dollar of investment tends to be large. In the private sector the rather rapid expansion of manufacturing capacity that has occurred in a number of countries has tended to concentrate on consumer goods and assembly operations; and although this has meant extensive import replacement and foreign exchange savings for these items, it has also meant increased demand for machinery, spare parts, raw materials, and fuel, which had, in large part, to be imported. At the stage of development at which most Latin American countries find themselves, growth is difficult without an expansion of imports, and these countries are no exception.

Trade within Latin America is negligible. Not over ten per cent of Latin American exports go to other Latin American countries, and, although efforts are being made to encourage intra-American trade through the Central American Economic Integration Treaty, the Latin America Free Trade Association, and in other ways, the development of intraregional exchange is very slow. Latin American exports are mainly competitive rather than complementary, and the lack of currency convertibility makes it difficult to take advantage of whatever opportunities for trade triangulation may exist. There is no reason to expect that this situation will continue indefinitely. After all, the exports of the several States following the American Revolution were as noncomplementary as are Latin American exports now, and trade among the states was a small fraction of shipments overseas. But the development of intraregional trade in Latin America has a very long way to go, and, in the meantime, these countries will have to depend on imports from the United States and Western Europe.

By far the most important source of foreign exchange to pay for imports are export earnings, and, as we have seen, the United States is by far the largest importer of Latin American products. The U.S. share of both exports from and imports into Latin America has declined substantially since the mid-1950s as Western European markets and export capacity have increased rapidly. But the United States will undoubtedly continue in its predominant position, a position that has led one observer to say of Latin American countries, "Whenever difficulties arise with respect to prices received for their exports, the tendency is to put the entire onus upon the United States rather than upon the world market."[2] Certainly the United States is expected to do what it can in the area of commercial policy to stabilize and increase Latin American export earnings, and, consequently, trade policy becomes a potentially important element within the Alliance for Progress in promoting Latin American development.

[2] Reynold E. Carlson, "The Economic Picture," in The American Assembly, *The United States and Latin America* (New York, 1959). p. 123.

The areas of trade policy that appear to be of greatest concern to the Latin American countries are the following: discriminations against Latin American exports imposed particularly by the preferential systems of the British Commonwealth and the European Common Market; barriers to traditional Latin American exports imposed not only at the frontier but in the form of high internal taxes on the consumption of tropical products; the lack of preferential treatment for the manufactured exports of less developed countries as against similar exports from the developed countries; and, most importantly, international arrangements for stabilizing and increasing the price of various export commodities. To the extent that Latin American export earnings could be increased by action in any or all of these areas it would, of course, relieve the pressure for increased foreign aid.

All of these areas of trade interest are emphasized in the Charter of Punta del Este and its appended resolutions. The discussions under the auspices of the General Agreement on Tariffs and Trade (GATT) of the so-called "Kennedy round" have on the agenda the question of preferential treatment (nonreciprocal tariff reductions) for exports from less developed countries. And the United Nations Conference on Trade Policy scheduled for 1964, in the preparations for which Latin American participants have been very active, is expected to examine all feasible ways of increasing the export earnings of the underdeveloped world. Recent calculations indicate that if the underdeveloped world as a whole had paid 1958 prices for their 1962 imports, they would have benefited to the extent of $200 million; and that if they had received 1958 prices for their 1962 exports, they would have benefited to the extent of $1,400 million. Trade and trade policy as an instrument of development is much to the fore, and perhaps the central issue, as the Latin Americans see it, is how can the international division of labor be restructured in the interests of the less developed countries of the world.

It is impossible, within the scope of this chapter, to do justice to this range of issues. Our primary concern is the relation of trade to aid in the context of the Alliance for Progress. What can and should the United States do in the area of trade policy to promote economic development in Latin America, and how is this likely to affect the requirements for economic assistance? We have a common interest with Latin American countries in reducing the discrimination involved in the preferential system of the British Commonwealth and the European Common Market. Our primary concern is the discrimination against U.S. manufactured products. The Latin American concern is primarily with the discrimination against their raw material exports to Britain and Western Europe. But we also would benefit from increased Latin American exports to Western Europe since a high percentage of their foreign exchange earnings are spent in the United States. There is every reason to make common cause with Latin America in seeking a reduction of these discriminations. It does not follow, however, that we can do much about these arrangements of long standing which, moreover, enjoy the blessing of GATT. It might be possible to use the leverage of our large foreign aid programs in India and Pakistan to dislodge these countries from Commonwealth preference. But it is far from clear that to do so would be in our long-run interest, or of any benefit to Latin America.

With respect to nonpreferential barriers to traditional Latin American exports, the United States does not appear in a particularly favorable light. We drastically limit oil imports, including oil from Latin America. We have, on occasion, imposed quantitative limitations to imports of lead, zinc, and copper. We have, sometimes for health reasons, imposed barriers to the importation of Argentine beef. If Argentina and Brazil should exploit to the full their comparative advantage in the production of beef cattle, it is doubtful whether they would find an open market in the United States. We have traditionally imposed a high tariff on wool, which particularly affects Uruguay and Argentina. All these barriers need to be re-examined in the light of our participation in the Alliance for Progress. It would, however, take a bold prognosticator to foresee rapid progress here.

Internal taxes limiting the consumption of tropical products are heaviest in Western Europe. Recent trends have been toward a lowering of these taxes, and there is some reason to believe that this trend will continue. Coffee, sugar and cocoa would probably be the chief beneficiaries among Latin American exports, but here, of course, these exports meet competition from within preferential trading areas.

The underdeveloped world, including Latin America, has been pressing strongly for nonreciprocal reductions by developed countries of tariffs on manufactured products. It is plausibly argued that without preferential entry, at least for a period of time, such exports are unlikely to be able to meet the competition of established manufacturing enterprises in the developed world. As I suggested in Chapter 3, such an unreciprocated reduction is unlikely to come about except by concerted action. But such a proposal has been put forward for discussion in the "Kennedy round" and it should, and presumably will, receive the full support of the United States. Latin American countries have evinced little interest in this proposal presumably because it is to be discussed under the aegis of GATT, which is regarded as an outworn instrument of the industrial countries interested in maintaining the existing pattern of world trade in which the underdeveloped world exports raw materials and the developed world exports manufactured products. They prefer to put their faith in the United Nations Conference scheduled for 1964, which they hope will find a way to restructure world trade on the basis of a "dynamic" future look at comparative advantages rather than an existing "static" examination.

Although a diversification of exports from the underdeveloped world in the direction of manufactured products must come about if this world is to attain satisfactory growth, it would have to be said that Latin America has lagged behind in this development. Not more than ten per cent of total exports from the underdeveloped world now consists of manufactured products, and no Latin American country is to be found among the principal exporters, despite the fact that Brazil, Argentina and Mexico, at least, are among the most highly industrialized countries in the underdeveloped world. This may indicate that industrialization in Latin America has too heavily concentrated on indiscriminate import replacement behind excessive tariff barriers rather than on a selective cultivation of industries offering, at some stage, export possibilities. In any case, it suggests that developing an export market for manufactures is not entirely a matter of removing import barriers in the developed countries.

This brings us to the subject of commodity arrangements, which has for decades been high on the list of Latin American trade preferences. As I pointed out in Chapter 3, if the purpose of commodity arrangements is to raise the level of commodity prices rather than merely to stabilize fluctuations around a trend, they should properly be regarded as a form of aid. The aid is financed by higher prices to consumers rather than by higher taxes for taxpayers. The United States has a certain "burden sharing" interest in this form of aid to the extent that U.S. consumption of the commodity "stabilized" is less than our share of aid rendered in some other way. On the other hand, this type of aid would go only to countries producing the commodity under agreement in proportion to their share of total exports. It would appear excessively difficult to negotiate commodity agreements in such a way as to provide anything like the present relative shares of aid to aid-receiving countries. Furthermore, such aid would presumably be rendered without bargaining for a *quid pro quo* in the shape of self-help measures to assist economic development. This might or might not be a disadvantage.

The Latin American countries are clearly now more interested in the level of prices than in their stability. In the case of certain recent sharp declines in export earnings brought about, for instance, by a fall in the prices of Chilean copper or Brazilian coffee, the Export-Import Bank has shown a willingness to step in with sizable loans. The International Monetary Fund, also, sees such occasions as providing justification for the exercise of drawing rights. This method of handling the situation leaves the Latin American countries with a debt burden; but, if price declines are in fact variations below the long-term trend, they will presumably be followed by variations above the trend which, at least, present the possibility of liquidating debt burdens. Whether or not this is a satisfactory method of dealing with fluctuations in exchange earnings, Latin American interest, stimulated by recent declines in the terms of trade, is much more in the level than in the stability of commodity prices.

As one looks at Latin American commodity exports, however, it becomes doubtful whether the United States can do much more than it is now doing or contemplating. Half of those exports, by value, consist of oil and minerals. Production is mainly in the hands of firms at least as interested in higher prices as the producing countries and frequently capable of doing something about it. Here, the problem of Latin American governments is one of securing an adequate share of the proceeds. In the cases of oil and of copper, where the Chilean tax amounts to some 80 per cent of the net income of copper producers, they seem to have succeeded; perhaps, in fact, too well. Other exports, such as wheat, wool, or beef, run into the problem of competition from domestic sources in the importing country or from alternative sources not likely to be covered by agreements. A recent examination of the possibilities for international commodity agreements pretty much narrows the range, so far as Latin American exports are concerned, to coffee, cocoa, sugar, and possibly bananas. We have already distributed the former import quotas of Cuban sugar to the advantage of a number of Latin American countries. We are now members of an international coffee agreement and are considering participation in a cocoa agreement.[3]

This represents a substantial change in U.S. policy which, until recently, except for wheat and sugar, has been opposed to supporting the international price of raw materials. This change, it is fair to say, has been undertaken with considerable misgivings concerning the practicability of such arrangements. No such arrangements, to the best of my knowledge, has ever met success-

[3] The cocoa negotiations broke down in October 1963 over a difference of opinion between producing and consuming countries on the question of price. Whether and when negotiations will be resumed is not yet clear.

fully the problem of reducing output and exports from high-cost sources in favor of increasing output and exports from low-cost sources, particularly new ones. Under these circumstances the arrangement becomes a support for the *status quo* until such time as it is overwhelmed by pressures from low-cost sources inside or outside the agreement or from synthetic substitutes, and from consuming countries anxious to take advantage of these opportunities. Although there does not seem to be much long-term future for such agreements, it may well be that, for a time, coffee and cocoa agreements could bring Latin American exporters a somewhat higher price than they otherwise could expect.

As one surveys the prospect for changes in trade policy favorable to Latin American export earnings, one must conclude that no revolutionary improvement is in the offing. Recent changes in U.S. policy concerning commodity arrangements may offer some short-run advantage. There is also a real possibility that within the next few years concerted action on the part of the industrialized countries will provide preferential entry to manufactured exports from less developed countries. To take advantage of these opportunities, however, will require more realistic exchange rates in Latin America, and a greater concentration in industries with export possibilities than has hitherto been evident. The United States has a strong obligation, under the Alliance for Progress, as well as a strong interest, in supporting changes in trade policy favorable to Latin American export earnings. But it is improbable that improvements in this area will, over the next few years, sharply diminish the need for public capital flows.

𝕾𝕾𝕾

FOREIGN private investment is another potentially important source of financing for Latin American economic development, and a few words need to be said concerning its probable role within the framework of the Alliance for Progress. As I have already pointed out, the stake of United States investors in Latin America is large, particularly in comparison with their interests in the rest of the underdeveloped world. At the end of 1962, U.S. private investment in Latin America was valued at $12,190 million, of which $8,472 million was direct investment. But, as I also pointed out, net U.S. capital flows to Latin America have been declining rapidly and reached a negative figure of $32 million in 1962. It should be noted, however, that the reinvestment of earnings of American firms in Latin America totaled $287 million in 1962.[4] The decline of net capital flow in recent years, and current prospects for private investment in Latin America, raise serious doubts as to whether the $300 million a year counted on from U.S. private investors in making up the $2 billion of capital inflow deemed necessary to finance the Alliance program can be realized.

It would have to be said that the Charter of Punta del Este does not place a heavy emphasis on the role of foreign private investment. It is said in Chapter IV of that document, on External Assistance in Support of National Development Programs, that, "The economic and social development of Latin America will require a large amount of additional public and private financial assistance on the part of capital-exporting countries . . ." But this is the only mention in the Charter of foreign private investment. It is declared to be an Alliance objective, "To stimulate private enterprise in order to encourage the development of Latin American countries at a rate which will help them to provide jobs for their growing populations. . . ." But nothing is said about foreign private enterprise. There are numerous resolutions concerned with education, public health, taxation, programming, and the like, but none devoted to the conditions propitious to the flow of foreign private funds.

Nor, during the first year of the Alliance, was any particular

---

[4] These figures are taken from the *Survey of Current Business,* August, 1963.

stress put upon foreign private investment. The emphasis in Latin American statements was on the expected flow of public funds from the United States. The emphasis in American statements was on the need for development planning and for self-help measures and social reforms designed to increase local resources available for development and to improve the well-being of the masses.

It required the impetus provided by the rather drastic decline in foreign investment mentioned above, and substantial evidence of a sizable flight of domestic capital from Latin America, to turn the attention of the Alliance to this problem. Accurate information on the volume of capital flight is lacking, but reliable observers think it may have reached an annual level of from $500 million to $800 million. If this is so, the adverse effect on the Latin American balance of payments of the decline in new foreign investment, plus the export of domestic capital, may have exceeded the beneficial effect of the flow of U.S. public funds during the first year of the Alliance.

Secretary Dillon forcibly brought this matter to the fore in his statement at the first annual review of the Alliance in Mexico City, October 1962:

There is one area in which during the past year we have not only made no progress but where we have suffered a serious setback. Private investment, both domestic and foreign, has suffered damaging blows and has lost confidence. Not only has foreign private investment in Latin America declined, but private domestic capital has been seeking safe havens outside Latin America. This capital flight has in some cases reached serious proportions.

The plain fact of the matter is that private enterprise has not always been made to feel that it is truly a part of the Alliance.[5]

Whatever the influence of this admonition in Latin America, there is no doubt that in the United States it has received atten-

[5] *Report of the First Annual Review of the Alliance for Progress.* Pamphlet for the use of the Committee on Foreign Affairs, House of Representatives. p. 5.

tion. Earlier in 1962 the Secretary of Commerce had established a Commerce Committee on the Alliance for Progress, composed of leading businessmen with interests in Latin America. The Report of the Clay Committee laid heavy emphasis on the role of private enterprise in economic development. The President, in recommending to Congress the Foreign Aid Bill for 1963, said that "the primary new initiative in this year's program relates to our increased efforts to encourage the investment of private capital in the underdeveloped countries. . . ."[6] And, within AID, under the vigorous Assistant Administrator for Development Finance and Private Enterprise, increased attention is being given to the promotion of U.S. private investment in Latin America. It remains to be seen, however, in the absence of effective co-operation of the Latin American partners in the Alliance for Progress, how much can be accomplished in this area.

Apart from tax incentives and loans from the Export-Import Bank, most of the devices for promoting U.S. private investment abroad are now administered by AID. These include participation with U.S. firms in the financing of investment surveys, dollar loans to private investors ineligible for Export-Import Bank borrowing, loans from P.L. 480 local currency, and a broad range of investment guarantees. It is impossible to estimate the net effect of these aids on net investment, but it would seem that the government has gone about as far as it can go to promote U.S. private foreign investment in Latin America without outright subsidization.

The action of American firms in adapting themselves to the changing situation has probably been of greater importance in sustaining foreign private investment in Latin America than anything the government could do for them. They have trained and promoted local officials to high positions; they have taken the lead

6 On business reactions to the Alliance for Progress and the role of private enterprise in economic development, Emilio G. Collado, "Economic Development Through Private Enterprise," *Foreign Affairs*, July, 1963, at p. 715.

in the provision of housing and social services to their employees; they have actively sought out local suppliers; and they have increasingly invited the participation of local capital, although in the area of joint ventures they have lagged behind the goals favored by the U.S. government. One of the most interesting and successful private attempts to encourage both domestic and foreign private investment has been the activities of the Creole Investment Corporation in undertaking minority equity investment in Venezuelan enterprises. Another promising venture is the Atlantic Community Development Group for Latin America, initiated by Senator Javits and European colleagues, which is expected to channel equity capital from Western Europe and the United States into the private sector in Latin America. Altogether, we have come a long way from the era of Banana Republics.

And yet, foreign private investment lags. To understand why this is so, the scene has to be shifted to Latin America. It would be fruitless at this point to undertake a rehearsal of the arguments for and against the proper role of foreign private investment in economic development. In my own view, it could make a large contribution, particularly in Latin America. But the questions that primarily concern us here are how large a contribution will it be allowed to make in view of Latin American attitudes and policies and what, if anything, can be done to improve the prospects for foreign private investment within the Alliance for Progress.

Traditionally, the two areas in which foreign investment in Latin America has been large have been public utilities and the extractive industries. Since the war, there has been a substantial flow of U.S. private funds into manufactures, particularly to Mexico and Brazil. This flow continues despite the drying up of investment in other areas. In 1962, when U.S. foreign investment as a whole in Latin America reached a negative figure, there was still a net investment of $114 million in manufactures.

During the nineteenth and early twentieth centuries, the flow of private investment funds into Latin American utilities, both from Europe and the United States, was large. Given the whole history of this investment, marked by numerous repudiations and expropriations, it is doubtful whether it yielded a positive return.[7] It should be clear, by now, that public utility investment within the context of the typical Latin American inflationary process is a losing game. Although the capital requirements for overhead facilities continue to be large and the foreign exchange content high, such foreign funds as are available are exclusively from public lending agencies and from this source only if the debt becomes an obligation of the borrowing government. Certainly, as an area of foreign private investment, public utilities can be removed from further consideration.

The largest area of U.S. private investment in Latin America is, of course, in the extractive industries. Here the prospects for increased investment are problematical. On the one hand, the Latin American governments have made it clear that they want to hold this investment to a minimum. On the other hand, the foreign demand for oil and most minerals is rising rapidly, the capital requirements are large, and it is difficult to dispose of outputs in the absence of distributing organizations in the raw material consuming countries. Latin American opinion and government action have left no doubt that this type of foreign investment is viewed with disfavor. The Mexican government now grants a 50 per cent tax rebate to mining companies with 51 per cent, or more, Mexican ownership. Brazil has long forbidden exploration by foreign oil companies, and has recently eased out an American iron ore mining operation. The reversal of policy in Argentina which permitted private oil exploration has met with widespread political opposition and, in fact, the reversal has recently been declared unconstitutional. How far abrogations of contracts made under the Frondizi government will be carried and what compensation, if any, will be offered is unclear as this

[7] The British experience has been recently reviewed by J. Fred Rippy, *British Investments in Latin America, 1882–1949* (Minneapolis, 1959).

is written. Chile has taxed the U.S. copper companies up to 81 per cent of net income, and whether the tax situation will be adjusted to permit new investment is still under consideration. Attractive opportunities for investment exist in Bolivia or, rather, would exist given similar treatment to foreigners as Bolivia gives to its own nationals. Of the extractive industries as a whole, it would have to be said that while the investment opportunities could be large, it is doubtful whether they will generate any sizable net flows of foreign private funds.

While the prospects are more favorable in manufacture, the total U.S. investment in this field in Latin America is still small as compared with the investment in extractive industries. At the end of 1962 it amounted to $1,900 million. This investment is there mainly to produce for the local market. Its orientation is very similar to that of domestic manufacturing investment, i.e., in the direction of import replacement. If U.S. manufacturers are flexible in their adjustment to the local scene, willing to accept local partners, developing products not yet locally produced, responsive to the attitude of local competitors where they exist, and willing to blend into the environment, then there is no reason to think that investment opportunities will not continue to be good. As Latin American incomes rise, the market for goods that American producers are accustomed to produce will rise proportionately. Nevertheless, it cannot be denied that there is a growing hostility to foreign investment, even in the manufacturing area, not only from left-wing intellectuals, but also from the business community. This will probably increase as local businessmen emerge as competitors to foreign entrepreneurs. Vernon has remarked on this attitude in Mexico, but it exists elsewhere in Latin America, also.[8] It is a mistake to think that a Latin American blessing of private enterprise, where this is forthcoming, also necessarily embraces foreign private enterprise.

[8] See Raymond Vernon, *The Dilemma of Mexico's Development* (Cambridge, Mass., 1963).

It would be foolhardy in this uncertain situation to forcast the flow of net U.S. private investment to Latin America. Yet I confess I would be surprised to see it touch, within the next few years, the $300 million a year envisaged by the Alliance for Progress. To evaluate the contribution of private investment to Latin American development only in terms of the net flow of funds from outside is, of course, highly misleading. Reinvestment of earnings of U.S. firms approximates $300 million per annum and this, plus investment of depreciation allowances, brings with it new equipment, new techniques, and a valuable complement of technical assistance. But despite this, it seems unlikely that foreign private investment will fill the role the United States would like to see it play in the Alliance for Progress.

Can anything be done about this, either by the United States or by the Latin American governments, within the context of the Alliance? The United States Congress has already intervened in a negative sort of way to protect U.S. private investments by enacting the Hickenlooper amendment referred to briefly in Chapter 2. As one might expect, this amendment has not been greeted with favor in Latin America or elsewhere in the underdeveloped world. The Brazilian ambassador to the United States, Roberto de Oliveira Campos, one of the most respected of Latin American officials, put the case against the Hickenlooper amendment as follows:

Such a provision, unless wisely administered, may become a source of interminable friction in United States relations with the Latin American countries, which are likely to question (a) the implied assumption that compensation in convertible foreign exchange is required under international law when legal tradition supports only the requirement that compensation be made in a "useful" form of payment; (b) the premature internationalization of disputes, in view of the fact that, unless and until denial of justice by local courts is demonstrated, litigation between individual companies and sovereign states remains a matter of internal and not international law; and (c) the possibility that foreign assistance programs may be transformed into a dangerous leverage by private interests in support of exaggerated claims on foreign governments.[9]

This is a good legal argument, and it is more than a mere legal argument in the sense that without wise administration the Hickenlooper amendment could create interminable friction and could be used to support exaggerated private claims. The argument on the other side is that American taxpayers can hardly be asked to shoulder the burden of financing a flow of public funds made appreciably heavier by the unwillingness of Latin American governments to tolerate foreign private investments and that, in particular, they should not be asked to finance the expropriation of American firms. The issues that have arisen in Latin America have concerned Dr. Campos' country and, on the whole, the amendment seems to have been wisely administered. Its existence will probably serve as a strong deterrent to incautious action, and, without such a deterrent, it is doubtful how far U.S. opinion would continue to support a large outflow of public funds.

Can and should the foreign aid program be further used to promote U.S. private investment in Latin America? It is taken for granted that the foreign office of any country supports the legitimate claims of citizens abroad to the best of its ability. And, despite the frequent complaints of U.S. businessmen concerning the lukewarmness or incompetence of State Department support, there is no evidence that it is less forthcoming than the support by other governments of their citizens abroad. The possible uses of foreign aid as an instrument go further than this. Should foreign aid be withheld or conditioned on particular treatment for U.S. investors? To do so, except in egregious cases of inequity, would seem to me to tread on dangerous ground. We are concerned in the Alliance for Progress, and in our aid program in

[9] "Relations Between the United States and Latin America," in Mildred Adams (ed.), *Latin America: Evolution or Explosion* (New York, 1963), pp. 49, 50.

general, with a much broader and deeper range of interests. These could easily be sacrificed by a narrow concern for U.S. private investment, even though we are convinced that private investment makes an important contribution to economic development.[10]

[10] Many of the issues involved in the use of aid as an instrument to protect and promote U.S. private investment are illustrated by the situation of the American copper companies in Chile. Two companies, Anaconda and Kennecott, account for over 90 per cent of Chilean copper production, and copper exports account for nearly 70 per cent of Chilean foreign exchange earnings. In 1955, the companies jointly negotiated a tax agreement with the Chilean government that provided for a basic tax of 50 per cent of net income and a supplementary tax of 25 per cent which was reducible in proportion to expansion of output. By 1960, Anaconda's total tax liability had been reduced to 60 per cent of net income though Kennecott's was somewhat higher. In 1961, the agreement of 1955 was abrogated by the imposition of two new taxes at 8 per cent and 5 per cent of net income. This raised Kennecott's tax obligation to 81 per cent and Anaconda's to a somewhat lower figure. The companies maintain that at this level investment is unprofitable but that they stand willing to make large investments at a more reasonable level of taxation guaranteed over a sufficient period of time.

The companies' case has been argued vigorously and at length by the U.S. government in Santiago and in Washington. The question that concerns us is whether the leverage of aid can and should be brought into use. Specifically, should fair and equitable tax treament of the copper companies be made a condition of aid along with the conditions agreed to in connection with a stabilization program? On the one hand, it can be argued that an increase in foreign exchange earnings is necessary to Chilean development; that the only large and readily available source of increased earnings is an expansion of copper exports; that such an expansion of exports requires a large increase in investment; and that a failure to make such an increase possible simply shifts the burden to U.S. taxpayers who are asked to finance public loans and grants to Chile. On the other hand, that two foreign companies account for 70 per cent of Chile's foreign exchange earnings and that the tax returns from these companies amount to perhaps 15 per cent of Chilean government revenues gives these companies high political visibility. Attacking the copper companies is an established route to political power in Chile, and this route is by no means travelled exclusively by left-wing partisans. The additional taxes in 1961 were imposed by the conservative party then and now in power. And in general, the conservative element in Chile, while extremely resistant to anything in the nature of domestic reform, is quite willing

In sum, the United States would like to envisage a large role for foreign private investment as an instrument of Latin American development within the framework of the Alliance for Progress. To this end, the government has devised and administers an impressive array of incentives to induce private investment. American business, furthermore, exhibits an increased willingness to adapt itself to local conditions. Nevertheless, investment lags primarily because foreign private investors do not find the current climate in Latin America particularly congenial. There is probably not very much the United States can do by itself to improve this climate, even with the leverage of a large foreign assistance program. If foreign private investment is to play the part envisioned for it in the Alliance for Progress, the principal responsibility for action would appear to be lodged in Latin America.

♫♫♫

IT HAS been emphasized that an essential condition of economic development in Latin America is increased access to imports. For various reasons discussed above, it appears unlikely that the necessary increase will be provided, at least within the next few years, either by higher export receipts or by an increased flow of private investment. But it has also been emphasized that increased capacity to import is not enough. Self-sustaining growth in Latin America is unlikely to be attained without increased investment and a better use of domestic resources. This may require changes in fiscal, monetary, and exchange policies and in budgetary prac-

---

to join in any attempt to lay Chile's burden on the foreigners. Under these circumstances, it seems highly dubious whether equitable tax treatment of the copper companies could or should be considered as a condition of aid.

tice, and it may also require far-reaching institutional reforms.

The Alliance for Progress recognizes the double-sided nature of the problem and proposes an ambitious cooperative method for dealing with it. The primary initiative for the Alliance came from Latin America, and the Charter of Punta del Este represents only the most recent in a long series of steps to achieve concerted action in Latin America in dealing with questions of economic development and political and social reform. It is a series to which the Economic Commission for Latin America, the various existing and proposed free trade areas, President Kubitschek's Operation Pan America, and the Committee of Twenty One, whose final product was the Act of Bogotá, have all made contributions. United States policy had also been moving slowly but perceptibly away from unilateral action and exclusively bilateral dealings toward the goal of more serious regional cooperation.

The Alliance is, in many ways, a remarkable conception. As Alberto Lleras Camargo, former President of Colombia, emphasizes,

Neither the Charter of Punta del Este nor the Declaration to the Peoples of America, which preceded it, nor any of the annexed resolutions, has the formal character of ordinary international agreements, covenants and treaties. . . . The governments bind themselves, not so much to the other signatory nations as to their own peoples, to carry out a policy which will, in effect, be the product of the closest international collaboration. Any of the 20 states may, without previous notice, withdraw from the Alliance simply by communicating the fact. Any state, moreover, may renounce the economic, political and social principles agreed upon in the various documents. The Punta del Este agreements, then, are no mere diplomatic instruments, but the final adoption of a great conjoint policy which is itself the result of a deep collective conviction.[11]

The Alliance does not rely on treaty obligations or formal commitments. Nor is the organizational and administrative machinery,

---

[11] Alberto Lleras Camargo, "The Alliance for Progress: Aims, Distortions, Obstacles," *Foreign Affairs*, October, 1963, p. 26.

designed to achieve a common course of action and to execute it, very extensive or, to date, very impressive. A Committee of Nine was established as a group of impartial experts (seven Latin Americans, one from the United States, and one from Europe) to appraise the proposed economic and social development programs of Latin American countries and to act as arbitrators between the sources and the recipients of funds. Beyond this, the Alliance relies on an annual meeting of the Inter-American Economic and Social Council to review its progress and propose new courses of action. The Council is a subordinate body of the Organization of American States, and it would have to be said that the O.A.S. does not enjoy high prestige in the United States and even less in Latin America. The Administrator of the Alliance for Progress in Washington does not have a Latin American counterpart, nor does he have a chief representative in Latin America. The Inter-American Development Bank is located in Washington as, of course, is the Export-Import Bank, the World Bank, the I.M.F., and other sources of funds. Such administrative machinery as the Alliance possesses is markedly oriented toward the United States.

In the absence of formal commitments and any very extensive machinery, the Alliance must perforce depend heavily on a recognition of common goals and of shared purpose. In the words of Roberto Campos, the Alliance "is a work of social engineering, requiring from the people a passionate involvement. In this sense it has to act as counter-myth to the Communist ideology which, despite its wanton brutality, has been rather successful in conveying to neglected masses a feeling of participating in the construction of new societies."[12] And Governor Muñoz Marín of Puerto Rico has said, "The ideals of the Alliance must be fused with the national ideals of each country." In the words of Lincoln Gordon, our Ambassador to Brazil, "A political mystique is indispensable to the success of the Alliance for Progress and . . .

[12] Cited, p. 55.

leadership in the creation of this political mystique must come from Latin America."[13]

It is to be doubted, however, whether mystique is enough, or rather, whether the proper mystique can be developed without a closer involvement in common decision-making than the Alliance has been able to achieve thus far. In this connection it may be useful to refer to the experience of the Marshall Plan, our only previous venture in regional administration of aid. There is no doubt that the Marshall Plan developed a mystique, but this emerged through a set of arrangements and practices very different from those now visible in the Alliance for Progress. I believe that the Alliance must work toward something like the Marshall Plan arrangements both in Washington and in Latin America, though this is likely to be a rather slow process.

It is frequently pointed out that the problems of the Alliance are very much more difficult than those of the Marshall Plan in the sense that (a) the need in Europe was for a flow of imports for a period of time long enough to restore the export earning capacities of economies capable in all other respects of sustained growth, while in Latin America many other conditions for sustained growth need to be fulfilled; and (b) Western Europe had a well-developed managerial class both in the public and private sectors, while this exists in Latin America to a markedly smaller degree. Both of these differences are real and important, but they are not in themselves insuperable barriers to the development over time of an effective regional organization.

The organizational differences between the Marshall Plan and the Alliance for Progress are very great both in Washington and in the field. Marshall Plan assistance was administered through an independent operating agency, the Economic Cooperation Administration, which looked to the State Department only for the most general policy guidance. There was no P.L. 480 program or Peace Corps lying outside its jurisdiction, and the Export-

[13] Lincoln Gordon, *A New Deal for Latin America: The Alliance for Progress* (Cambridge, 1963), p. 111.

Import Bank was not lending in Europe. The independent status of the agency and the novelty and importance of the task made it possible to attract some of the ablest Americans to senior positions, and the quality of its staff has rarely been equalled by government agencies. Trade and monetary policy were an integral part of the assistance operation and although E.C.A. met with opposition from the State Department and the Treasury, is was strong enough to carry through a thoroughly regional program for Western Europe. Of course, the building up of a European trade and payments union discriminating heavily against American exports would have been impossible—nor would it have been attempted—in the absence of our overwhelming balance-of-payments surplus.

In contrast, the organization for the Alliance for Progress in Washington is a loose attempt to coordinate the activities of a large number of independent agencies each with its own point of view and special interests. The position of the Administrator is one of much responsibility and little power. The initiative for trade policy is with the State Department, and although we have modified our attitude toward commodity agreements with Latin American interests very much in mind, there is no disposition, as in the days of the Marshall Plan, to depart very far from traditional trade practices in favor of regional interests. The authority for P.L. 480 disposals lies with the Secretary of Agriculture, and the Peace Corps is an independent agency. The Export-Import Bank, which is a large lender in Latin America, may be influenced but is certainly not controlled by the Administrator of the Alliance for Progress. Actions in Washington affecting the Alliance are the product of a large number of interagency committees on which the Administrator is represented along with the spokesmen for many other interests. Under these circumstances, Washington finds it difficult to speak with one voice in affairs concerning the Alliance.

But it is in the organizational arrangements outside of Washington that the Marshall Plan contrasts most strongly with the Alliance. The European centerpiece of the Marshall Plan was the

Organization for European Economic Cooperation which not only provided a frequent meeting place for responsible ministers of state, but possessed a large and highly qualified staff of civil servants working continuously on problems of European recovery. The United States participated *de jure* in O.E.E.C. activities only as an observer; but, *de facto,* Ambassador Harriman, the first chief E.C.A. representative in Europe, and his large staff in Paris participated fully in the formulation of recovery policies. In the course of time, the staff of O.E.E.C. and their American counterparts came to regard themselves more as international civil servants than as representatives of particular countries, and the mystique of the Marshall Plan grew out of this intimate collaboration.

The United States came to depend on O.E.E.C. for the annual estimate of country requirements. This estimate was, of course, not binding, but it was accepted in Washington with relatively few modifications. It was hammered out in a process of give-and-take in which U.S. representatives participated, and it inevitably involved a large measure of intervention in what are normally regarded as the domestic affairs of the member countries. Marshall Plan aid was quite definitely not "aid without strings." The conditions in the form of sensible economic policies and practices in the receiving countries involved extensive intervention, but it was mainly intervention via the deliberations of a European organization with American participation rather than via bilateral negotiations.

One of the major reasons why an organization like O.E.E.C. was possible in Europe and is not, at least at this juncture, in Latin America is that in an economic sense Western Europe is much more of an integrated region than is Latin America. Before the war, the volume of intra-European trade was a large fraction of the total foreign trade of the area. These trade connections had been broken in the 1930s and during the war, and one of the most difficult problems facing O.E.E.C. was the establishment of multilateral clearing arrangements and the removal of commercial policy restrictions to intraregional trade. This was possible at all

only because of a common recognition on the part of the participating countries that unimpeded intraregional trade was a *sine
qua non* of recovery. The task was also facilitated by our rather
extraordinary complaisance toward a set of policies discriminating against the United States.

Nothing remotely resembling the O.E.E.C. has yet been established within the framework of the Alliance for Progress. The
task of the Committee of Nine is a very different one, namely to
facilitate bilateral negotiations between the United States as a
source of funds and individual Latin American countries which
present programs of economic and social development and give
evidence of adequate attempts to help themselves. There is a
growing recognition within the Alliance for Progress of the need
for a Latin American organization performing at least some of
the functions of O.E.E.C. and a realization that the Organization
of American States and its subordinate bodies will not serve this
purpose.[14] It can hardly be expected, at this juncture at least, that
such an organization could undertake the delicate task of formu-

---

14 At a meeting in Mexico City of the Inter-American Economic and
Social Council to review the first year of the Alliance for Progress, it
was agreed "to entrust to two outstanding citizens the study of the
current structure of the inter-American system as it relates to the
Alliance for Progress. . . ." This task was given to former President
Kubitschek of Brazil and former President Lleras of Colombia and in
June, 1963, these representatives submitted their separate reports to
the Council of the Organization of American States. Both of these
reports recommended the formation of an Inter-American Development Committee representing all the members of the O.A.S. but with
a smaller executive body devoting full time to the affairs of the
Alliance. Both recommended Washington as at least the initial seat of
the Committee, but it is suggested in the Kubitschek report that in
time the Committee, the Inter-American Development Bank and the
Committee of Nine should be based in some Latin American capital.
There are certain differences in the recommended composition of the
Committee and in the definition of its functions which were left for
the consideration of the Inter-American Economic and Social Council
at its meeting to review the second year of the Alliance for Progress.
It seems probable that some serious moves toward "Latinizing" the
Alliance and strengthening its capacity to act as a regional agency are
in process.

lating the financial requirements for development country by country. There is, however, increased awareness of the fact that the presentation of large claims for balance-of-payment support on the part of one country may well mean less in the form of development assistance for others. And it is quite possible that in the course of time Latin American pressure against the domestic policies that generate such claims can be more effective than tough bilateral bargaining.

As I have pointed out, the intraregional trade in Latin America is less than ten per cent of the total exports of the area. The close economic interdependence that gave meaning to much of the activity of O.E.E.C. is at present lacking. But this trade can develop with time, and it should be one of the interests of a Latin American arm of the Alliance to encourage it. Furthermore, there are strong regional ties deriving from language, culture, the rather similar course of political development, and a significant set of common organizations. Certainly, there are reasons for treating Latin America for development purposes as a region that do not apply to southern or eastern Asia or to Africa. But if the Alliance is to be conceived as a regional development organization, it is high time that Washington install machinery capable of producing a consistent set of policies relevant to Latin America and that the Latin American partners create an organization capable of understanding some of the repercussions on regional development of the actions of individual countries and doing something about it.

Doing something about it means intervention in the traditionally domestic concerns of countries. And intervention is an ugly word. There will be intervention in any case in the sense of conditions, more or less onerous, attached to aid. The only question is whether this intervention takes the form of persuasion and pressure generated within an organization of which all are members and in which all have a voice, or whether it is brought to bear in bilateral negotiations. If Latin America really is, or can be made, a region in a significant sense for development purposes, it seems probable that external influences on domestic policies can be both more effective and more acceptable if mediated by a regional organization.

The alternative for the United States and for the Latin American countries is periodic confrontation in which the Monetary Fund, the World Bank and possibly the D.A.C. may participate but in which the United States, as the principal creditor, essentially calls the turn. During the first year-and-a-half of the Alliance, this has in fact been the standard procedure. The Committee of Nine has exercised some influence as a mediator and has imparted a slight regional flavor, but, in the main, the Alliance has operated through tough bilateral negotiations. The results to date have not been very encouraging. The conditions for assistance to Brazil from the United States and other sources were a set of promised actions looking toward monetary stabilization. But the price level promises to rise in the neighborhood of 70 per cent in 1963. The conditions not having been fulfilled, most of the assistance is not forthcoming, and Brazil's financial position is highly precarious. Colombia, for reasons not entirely within its own control, is finding it impossible to meet the conditions on which large assistance commitments were made in 1962. Indeed, despite notable successes in particular areas and special programs, there are very few countries that have made substantive economic progress over-all during the first two years of the Alliance.

The fact is that the Alliance for Progress to date has not developed the capacity to act, in the words of Ambassador Campos, as a creditable "counter-myth to the Communist ideology." As one observes the military take-overs in Argentina, Peru, Ecuador, Guatemala, Honduras, and the Dominican Republic since the initiation of the Alliance, a rather different type of alternative to Communism appears to be emerging. It seems highly improbable that this kind of regime is a real alternative or that it can stand for long, though it is equally improbable that we have seen the last of such take-overs. Internal struggles for power arising from the sharp class cleavages and irreconcilable ideological differences characteristic of Latin America seem inevitable in a number of countries.

It does not follow, however, that because military dictatorship is usually not an effective alternative to Communism, there are no effective alternatives. The forces behind the Alliance in Latin America standing for a moderate, evolutionary and democratic approach to change are real and potent forces, and it is highly probable that the future belongs to them. The military regimes in Argentina and Peru have already surrendered power to democratically elected governments, and this is likely to happen elsewhere. It is strongly in our interest to support the forces behind the Alliance and it is very much in their interest to have the support of the United States. The economic difficulties confronting Latin American development can hardly be overcome without a substantial flow of public funds, principally from the United States. And the changes in domestic policy and, over time, the changes in domestic institutions in Latin America will certainly be easier if the external pressures come from a regional organization in which the Latin countries have an effective voice. Although the time schedule of the Alliance for Progress has been drawn too optimistically, the Alliance continues to represent the only approach to Latin American development that holds much promise for the future.

CONCLUSION

A DISCUSSION of the relation of foreign aid to foreign policy necessarily assumes that foreign aid programs are shaped to a substantial extent with the interests of the aid-dispensing countries in mind. I have seen no reason to doubt the validity of that assumption. There is, however, a considerable variety of interests influencing the amounts, the terms, and the form of aid within the aid-giving countries and among them. Domestic economic concerns, the promotion of foreign trade, and security interests vie for priority with a humanitarian desire for the well-being of others. In the United States this variety is suggested by the names of the agencies that, in one form or another, participate in foreign aid: the Agency for International Development, the Peace Corps, the Food for Peace Program, the Export-Import Bank, to mention only the principal participants. The changes over time in the title of the principal U.S. foreign assistance agency also suggest shifting purposes and, perhaps, a certain ambiguity of purpose. The Economic Cooperation Administration (E.C.A.) gave way to the Mutual Security Administration (M.S.A.) which, in turn, was followed by the International Cooperation Administration (I.C.A.) and, now, by the Agency for International Development (AID). There is a strong current of feeling in Washington that the initials of the present agency, AID, give an unfortunate and misleading interpretation of its real purposes; there is some disposition to return to a former name, Mutual Security Administration. Certainly the debates in Congress would indicate that mutual security is and should be the prime concern of our foreign assistance program.

Military assistance, a substantial part of defense support, and of expenditures from the contingency fund are obviously directed to security objectives. It is less clear what interests of the United States are served by economic development assistance. If such assistance is to be assessed in terms of its contribution to mutual security, it becomes necessary to form a judgment, first, on the extent to which external aid can, in fact, advance the economic development of less developed countries; and, second, on the question of what changes in political structure and behavior can be expected to accompany the process of economic development. Although the evidence is far from adequate, it is easier to arrive at a sensible judgment on the first question than on the second. Of a number of less developed countries to which aid flows in quantity, it can be said that access to foreign exchange is the limiting factor to economic growth. Some of these have already reached a stage of self-supporting development, and others are not far from attaining it. When, however, external assistance is only one of the conditions necessary for sustained growth, assessment of the contribution of aid becomes more difficult. There also intrudes the bothersome question of the extent to which the leverage of aid can and should be used to bring about changes in domestic policies considered to be propitious to economic development. Still, in the thirty-some less developed countries to which the bulk of U.S. economic aid is directed, it can be said with some confidence that the prospects of development are substantially improved by the availability of foreign assistance.

It does not follow from this that the less developed world is rapidly approaching a condition in which growth can be sustained without external assistance. In fact, it seems probable that in many countries to which we are heavily committed, a continuation of the growth rates of the recent past will require substantially more rather than less external assistance. Those to whom this is a distasteful, and even alarming, prospect would do well, however, to reflect on the difference between the nominal size of the aid burden now shouldered by developed countries and the real sacrifice it represents. When all the terms, limitations, and conditions surrounding the flow of aid are taken into account, the $6 billion a year estimate of the total flow of public funds from the advanced to less developed countries shrinks to a grant equivalent of perhaps $2.5 billion. This can hardly be considered a monumental sacrifice. If economic development assistance can and does in fact contribute to the emergence of a world in which it is somewhat easier for the developed countries in general, and the United States in particular, to live, it appears to be at small cost.

This, of course, is the crucial question that confronts any analysis of the relation of foreign aid to foreign policy. What can economic development, assuming it can be assisted by foreign aid, be expected to bring about in the area of political development and foreign policy in the aid-receiving countries? Is there in fact a social process called political development that can be described objectively and, if so, how is it related to economic growth? Economists, it is true, cannot tell us much about the origins or causes of economic development, nor can they attribute with conviction indubitable welfare consequences to economic growth. But they can offer a fair description of the economic development process in terms of a set of arrangements producing an increasing flow of consistently related inputs that over time will result in greater outputs of goods and services. And these inputs and outputs allow at least rough measurement.

Discussions of political development, on the other hand, customarily stress two significant strands of the process that do not appear to be necessarily related. One is concerned with an increasing ability of the organs of government to order human behavior to serve whatever goals the holders of political power choose to have served. If economic development is an important goal, ability of the government to govern is both a necessary condition and a consequence of economic growth. When General Ayub came to power in Pakistan in 1958, the direction of the activities of the citizenry was substantially increased, and the prospects of economic development commensurately improved. The second strand emphasized in discussions of political development is concerned with a broadening of public participation in the process of decision-making. Citizens whose voice is heard only in local affairs may over time come to be consulted in affairs of state. A government in which political power has rested in the hands of an elite may in the course of development enlarge the size of the group whose views are considered. This development may or may not lead toward parliamentary democracy. A single party system that, as in Mexico, provides for consultation of a wide spectrum of opinion may be deemed to be more politically advanced than a system closely controlled by a small group.

While there is some connection between the ability of a government to govern and the admission of the citizenry to consultation, the connection is obviously very complex. Some degree of consent of the governed is necessary to any effective ordering of human activities though there have been and are apparently efficient regimes relying heavily on force and terror. On the other hand, examples are not lacking of regimes in which a broadening participation of citizens in the process of government has been accompanied by a notable decline in the efficiency of government.

If foreign aid is to be used as an instrument of foreign policy and if the promotion of economic development is not an end in itself, what kind of political development in the aid-receiving country is sought to be achieved? Should assistance be denied to dictatorial regimes and be made available only to those governments capable of establishing their democratic bona fides? What if the democratic countries show themselves incapable of putting into practice the domestic policies essential to economic development and without which economic assistance is wasted? Reflection on these considerations in Latin America and elsewhere leads one to the opinion, I think, that doctrinaire views on the direction and use of foreign aid are unlikely to be effective. Under certain circumstances we may have to sacrifice a desire to promote a wider participation of the governed in order to preserve a modicum of effective government. On the other hand, it is clearly useless to try to support governments who assert their anticommunism but lack the effective support of their citizens.

ふふふ

THE MANUSCRIPT of this small volume was completed early in November 1963. Between that date and the present writing, late January 1964, a number of things have happened to the AID program. These include the Congressional vote on appropriations for fiscal year 1964 and the submission of the administration's budget request for fiscal 1965; the establishment of the Inter-American Committee on the Alliance for Progress; the appointment by President Johnson of a Special Assistant who is concurrently Assistant Secretary of State for Inter-American Affairs and U.S. Coordinator of the Alliance for Progress; and within the administration a serious reconsideration of the organization of the Agency for International Development.

Congress, eight months after the beginning of hearings and six months after the beginning of the fiscal year, voted AID appropriations of $3 billion for fiscal year 1964. This compares with $3.9 billion appropriated in the previous year and with $4,525 million requested by President Kennedy. Of the appropriation, $2 billion represent economic assistance and $1 billion, military assistance. Together with carryovers and recoveries from the previous year it makes possible an economic assistance program for fiscal year 1964 of $2,473 million. For fiscal year 1965 the President has requested $1 billion for military assistance and $2,392 million for economic aid. Together with expected carryovers and recoveries, this would provide programs for fiscal 1965 of about the same magnitude as for 1964. What effect the reduction in the size of the U.S. aid program will have on the contributions of other D.A.C. countries is problematic, but it seems certain that the persuasiveness of American arguments for an increase will, to say the least, be somewhat blunted.

At the meetings of the Inter-American Economic and Social Council in November 1963, it was voted to establish an Inter-American Committee on the Alliance for Progress. This Committee will consist of six members, of which one will be a permanent U.S. representative and five will be representatives on a rotating basis of Latin American countries. The Committee is intended to have an interlocking relationship with the Committee of Nine and will be served by the Secretariat of the Economic Section of the O.A.S. This action represents at least a beginning of an attempt to "Latinize" the Alliance for Progress. The President has also attempted to unify more effectively the U.S. contributions to the Alliance by appointing as his Special Assistant a joint Coordinator for the Alliance for Progress and Assistant Secretary of State for Inter-American Affairs.

In its report on the aid program for 1964 the Senate Committee on Foreign Relations suggested a thorough-going re-examination of the organization of AID before the submission of budget requests for fiscal year 1965. In response to this suggestion the President appointed a mainly governmental committee under the chairmanship of the Under-Secretary of State to examine the affairs of this much reorganized agency. After rejecting on the one hand a suggestion that the Agency be merged into the Department of State and, on the other, that it be broken into a number of parts (on the theory apparently that Congress would not be able to see the woods for the trees), the committee and President Johnson have settled for a further tightening up of the existing organization. *Plus ça change, plus c'est la même chose*— as indeed it must if AID is to continue to be an effective agency for economic development. It is, perhaps, time to recognize that U.S. foreign policy has serious responsibilities in the less developed world and that no amount of administrative sleight-of-hand or political hocus-pocus is likely to conjure them away.

INDEX

Act of Bogotá, 76, 98
Act of Chapultepec (1945), 74
Africa, 4, 29, 50, 53, 55, 56, 61
Agency for International Development (AID), 16, 21, 26, 35, 37, 38, 40, 42, 44, 46, 49, 54, 55n, 56, 66, 90, 107, 111, 112
Agricultural surpluses, 4, 5, 13, 15, 17, 26, 69; *see also* Public Law 480
Aid donors, interests of, 3–5, 46–47
Aid recipients, interests of, 3–5, domestic policies of, 47, 49; use of aid, 10
Aid tying, 13–14, 43
Alliance for Progress, 6, 7, 36, 43, Chap. 4 *passim*, 111, 112; Committee of Nine, 99, 103, 103n, 105; compared to Marshall Plan, 100–101; compared to O.E.E.C., 102–103; future of, 106; programs and purposes, 99
Appropriations: FY 1963, 16, 34, 111; FY 1964, 36, 111
Argentina, 72, 76, 77, 83, 84, 92, 93, 105, 106
Asia, 18, 50
Atlantic Community Development Group in Latin America, 91
Australia, 9, 67

Bell, David E., 38n, 54n
Bokaro Steel Mill, 44, 44n–46n
Bolivia, 72, 77

Brazil, 49, 72, 73, 76, 77, 83, 84, 91, 92
Burden sharing, 6, 9, 24, 25, 30, Chap. 3 *passim;* in D.A.C., 69–70; Europe, 55, 91; France, 6, 54, 55, 62, 69; geographical interests, 55–56; in I.D.A., 71; and mutual security, 54, 57, 66; NATO, 65–66, 68, and trade 62–64; United Kingdom, 55, 61, 68, 69; United States, 6, 19, 24

Campos, Roberto de Oliveira, 94, 95, 99, 105
Carlson, Reynold E., 81n
Central American Economic Integration Treaty, 81
Charter of Punta del Este, 82, 88, 98
Chile, 39, 76, 77, 105
China, Republic of, 39
Clay Committee, 18, 28, 34, 56, 58, 59, 90
Colombia, 72, 74, 76, 77, 105
Commerce Committee, U.S., Dept. of, on the Alliance for Progress, 90
Congo, 16, 23
Contingency fund, 16, 34, 35, 108
Creole Investment Corporation, 91
Costa Rica, 77
Cuba, 74, 76

Defense support, 20–21, 34, 35, 108
Denmark, 54
Development Assistance Committee (D.A.C.), 9, 11, 12, 14, 60, 67, 69, 70, 105, 111

International Cooperation Administration (I.C.A.), 107
International Development Association (I.D.A.), 23, 24, 36, 71
International Monetary Fund (I.M.F.), 23, 24, 47, 99, 105
Iran, 24
Iraq, 50
Israel, 39
Italy, 66

Japan, 4, 38, 46, 54, 56, 61, 64
Javits, Jacob, 91
Johnson, Lyndon B., 112
Jordan, 39

Kennedy, John F., 28, 76, 90
"Kennedy round," tariff negotiations, 63, 82
Korea, 40, 41, 68
Kubitschek, Juscelino, 75, 98, 103n

Latin America, 3, 7, 17, 43, 47, 50, 74, 112; Alliance for Progress, Chap. 4 passim; economic growth in, 76–77, 79; foreign private investment in, 78, 87–97; intraregional trade, 81, 104; and Kennedy administration, 76; obstacles to economic development, 78–79; and O.A.S., 74, 75; trade, 80–87, 97; trade with U.S., 72–73, 75, 81, 83, 86, 87; U.S. private investment in, 73–74, 75, 87–97
Latin America Free Trade Association, 81
Lebanon, 38
Lleras, Alberto Carmargo, 98, 98n, 103n
Loans, 5, 11, 12, 15, 16, 17, 21, 29, 30, 35, 36, 61, 68, 69, 70

Marshall Plan, 7, 8, 38, 50, 52, 53, 72, 75, 78, 100, 101, 102
McNamara, Robert S., 54
Mexico, 39, 72, 74, 76, 77, 79, 84, 91, 92, 93, 110

Military assistance, 16, 34, 54, 57, 59, 65–68; and mutual security, 4, 6, 10, 108; vs. economic assistance, 18–21
Monroe Doctrine, 74
Morgenthau, Hans, 31, 32, 32n, 33
Morrow, Dwight, 74
Muñoz Marín, Luis, 99
Mutual security: and burden sharing, 54, 57, 66; and defense expenditures, 6, 8; and economic aid, 6, 9, 10, 108; and military assistance, 4, 6, 10; as objective of aid, 3, 4, 31, 33
Mutual Security Administration (M.S.A.), 107
Myrdal, Gunnar, 28, 28n, 59

New Zealand, 9, 67
Nigeria, 56
Nixon, Richard, 76
North Atlantic Treaty Organization (NATO), 6, 54, 55, 56, 64, 65, 66, 68
Norway, 54

Operation Pan America, 75, 98
Organization for European Economic Cooperation (O.E.E.C.), 7, 102, 103, 104
Organization of American States (O.A.S.), 74, 75, 99, 103, 103n, 111; Committee of Twenty-One, 98
Organization of Economic Cooperation and Development (O.E.C.D.), 9, 13, 55, 56, 69

Pakistan, 20, 39, 41
Paraguay, 77
Peace Corps, 15, 16, 27, 36, 66, 100, 101, 107
Peru, 76, 77, 106
Point Four Program, 22
Political development, 6, 9, 11, 50–51, 109–110
Portugal, 29; aid as per cent of G.N.P., 12–13, 13n

Publications of the Council on Foreign Relations

FOREIGN AFFAIRS (quarterly), edited by Hamilton Fish Armstrong.

THE UNITED STATES IN WORLD AFFAIRS (annual). Volumes for 1931, 1932 and 1933, by Walter Lippmann and William O. Scroggs; for 1934–1935, 1936, 1937, 1938, 1939 and 1940, by Whitney H. Shepardson and William O. Scroggs; for 1945–1947, 1947–1948 and 1948–1949, by John C. Campbell; for 1949, 1950, 1951, 1952, 1953 and 1954, by Richard P. Stebbins; for 1955, by Hollis W. Barber; for 1956, 1957, 1958, 1959, 1960, 1961 and 1962, by Richard P. Stebbins.

DOCUMENTS ON AMERICAN FOREIGN RELATIONS (annual). Volume for 1952 edited by Clarence W. Baier and Richard P. Stebbins; for 1953 and 1954, edited by Peter V. Curl; for 1955, 1956, 1957, 1958 and 1959, edited by Paul E. Zinner; for 1960, 1961 and 1962, edited by Richard P. Stebbins.

POLITICAL HANDBOOK AND ATLAS OF THE WORLD (annual), edited by Walter H. Mallory.

AFRICA: A Foreign Affairs Reader, edited by Philip W. Quigg.

THE PHILIPPINES AND THE UNITED STATES: Problems of Partnership, by George E. Taylor.

SOUTHEAST ASIA IN UNITED STATES POLICY, by Russell H. Fifield.

UNESCO: ASSESSMENT AND PROMISE, by George N. Shuster.

THE PEACEFUL ATOM IN FOREIGN POLICY, by Arnold Kramish.

THE ARABS AND THE WORLD: Nasser's Arab Nationalist Policy, by Charles D. Cremeans.

TOWARD AN ATLANTIC COMMUNITY, by Christian A. Herter.

THE SOVIET UNION, 1922–1962: A Foreign Affairs Reader, edited by Philip E. Mosely.

THE POLITICS OF FOREIGN AID: American Experience in Southeast Asia, by John D. Montgomery.

SPEARHEADS OF DEMOCRACY: Labor in the Developing Countries, by George C. Lodge.

LATIN AMERICA: Diplomacy and Reality, by Adolf A. Berle.

THE ORGANIZATION OF AMERICAN STATES AND THE HEMISPHERE CRISIS, by John C. Dreier.

THE UNITED NATIONS: Structure for Peace, by Ernest A. Gross.

THE LONG POLAR WATCH: Canada and the Defense of North America, by Melvin Conant.

Publications of the Council on Foreign Relations

ARMS AND POLITICS IN LATIN AMERICA (Revised Edition), by Edwin Lieuwen.

THE FUTURE OF UNDERDEVELOPED COUNTRIES: Political Implications of Economic Development (Revised Edition), by Eugene Staley.

SPAIN AND DEFENSE OF THE WEST: Ally and Liability, by Arthur P. Whitaker.

SOCIAL CHANGE IN LATIN AMERICA TODAY: Its Implications for United States Policy, by Richard N. Adams, John P. Gillin, Allan R. Holmberg, Oscar Lewis, Richard W. Patch, and Charles W. Wagley.

FOREIGN POLICY: THE NEXT PHASE: The 1960s (Revised Edition), by Thomas K. Finletter.

DEFENSE OF THE MIDDLE EAST: Problems of American Policy (Revised Edition), by John C. Campbell.

COMMUNIST CHINA AND ASIA: Challenge to American Policy, by A. Doak Barnett.

FRANCE, TROUBLED ALLY: De Gaulle's Heritage and Prospects, by Edgar S. Furniss, Jr.

THE SCHUMAN PLAN: A Study in Economic Cooperation, 1950–1959, by William Diebold, Jr.

SOVIET ECONOMIC AID: The New Aid and Trade Policy in Underdeveloped Countries, by Joseph S. Berliner.

RAW MATERIALS: A Study of American Policy, by Percy W. Bidwell.

NATO AND THE FUTURE OF EUROPE, by Ben T. Moore.

AFRICAN ECONOMIC DEVELOPMENT, by William Hance.

INDIA AND AMERICA: A Study of Their Relations, by Phillips Talbot and S. L. Poplai.

JAPAN BETWEEN EAST AND WEST, by Hugh Borton, Jerome B. Cohen, William J. Jorden, Donald Keene, Paul F. Langer and C. Martin Wilbur.

NUCLEAR WEAPONS AND FOREIGN POLICY, by Henry A. Kissinger.

MOSCOW-PEKING AXIS: Strengths and Strains, by Howard L. Boorman, Alexander Eckstein, Philip E. Mosely and Benjamin Schwartz.

RUSSIA AND AMERICA: Dangers and Prospects, by Henry L. Roberts.

FOREIGN AFFAIRS BIBLIOGRAPHY, 1942–1952, by Henry L. Roberts.